Leading with Heart
Faith-Filled Thoughts on Leadership

Ken Hensley

© 2014 Ken Hensley

Table of Contents

Preface	6
What Size Is Your Life	8
Are You Hearing Multiple Voices?	9
Is Your Life A Candle Or A Torch	11
The Buck Stops Here	13
Peace And Thankfulness	15
What Are You Working Towards	17
Difficulties And Determination	19
Beyond Teamwork	21
Do You Have A Different Spirit	23
Are You Guarding Your Deposit	26
Calling Forth Potential	28
Investing In Shade Trees	30
Guarding Your Heart	32
Boss Or Leader	35
What Are You Pursuing	37
Good Leaders Inspire	39
Black Holes	41
Influence And Influenza	43
Displacement	45
For Or With	47
Telling Stories	49
Your Personal Battery	51
Why Good Leaders Are Good Communicators	53

Living In The Sweet Spot	55
Are You A Contributor Or Consumer?	57
Risk	59
Moving And Settling	61
Authentic Living – What's Missing	63
Insecurity Minimizes Potential	65
Do What You Love	67
Metabolizing A Situation	69
Setup For Success	71
Refocus, Recalibrate, Renew	73
White Space	75
Very Draining People	77
The Perspective Of Motivation	79
The Boys Will Be Home For Christmas	81
Kingdom Networking	83
Nimbleness	85
Where Ideas Die	87
Passion Regained	89
Preparing Your Horse	91
Comfort Or Cause	93
Reflections	95
Chasing Rabbits	97
More And Less	99
Success And Significance	101
That The Necessary May Speak	103
Compass Not A Clock	105

Humility	107
The Best Ideas	109
Leadership Agility	111
Something Special	113
Action And Despair	115
Duplicators Not Doers	120
Sundials In The Shade	122
What Else Is Not Enough	124
Adjustments And Alignment	126
Influence And Integrity	128
Fear Of Failing	130
Clarity And Communication	132
Shrinking Thinking	134
Simple Enough	136
Mobility	138
Courage	140
Developing Spiritual Wisdom	142
Watching And Listening	144
Great People, Great Passion	146
Carving Out The Angel	148
Leadership And Belief	150
Motivating Employees	152
Risk And Fear	154
Wannabee, Knowitall, Or Sponge	156
Vision Casting And Bubbling	158
How Can We Vs. Why Did You	160

Leadership Seasons	162
Are You Running Aimlessly?	164
Love What You Do and I Might Love It, Too	166
Leadership is Stewardship	170
Soaring with the Eagles	172
Chronic Inconsistency	174
Leaders Make Others Better	176
Learning to Lead	178
Incarnate or Duplicate?	180
Taking the High Road	183
Stopping the Downward Spiral	185
Keeping Things in Perspective	187
What's Next	189
About the Author	191

PREFACE

One of Newton's laws of physics states that for every action there is an equal and opposite reaction. Granted, that's a great oversimplification but what do you expect from a guy from Peoria?

Leaders would do well to pay attention to this law. Parents, too. And teachers and managers and coaches. Anyone in a position of influence should understand the law of action and reaction.

If it's true that we lead by example, that raises an obvious question: What kind of example are we setting? Your example — like it or not — is setting off a reaction inside those who follow you.

Where Newton's law breaks down when it comes to leadership influence is here: Not all reactions must be opposite in nature. In fact, good coaches bring out the best actions in their players. Positive parents inspire positive actions in their children.

But don't dismiss the main point: your actions are creating a reaction — either positive or negative. While you can't control how someone responds to your words or deeds, you can control your words and deeds. In that sense, you can influence the reaction to a certain degree.

For over twenty-five years I have been privileged to serve in positions of leadership. It is a privilege. Whenever someone willingly follows your leader, you have accepted a sacred responsibility – to lead well.

This book is a collection of posts that originally appeared on my blog (kenhensley.com). Though my main profession has been in professional ministry, they are written for leaders of all types. As such, they approach leadership from a Christian perspective. Regardless of your religious persuasion, I believe you will find them helpful.

Read on and lead well!

Ken Hensley
Highlands Ranch, CO
ken@kenhensley.com

WHAT SIZE IS YOUR LIFE

"There is no passion to be found playing small – in settling for a life that is less than the one you are capable of living." – Nelson Mandela

Are you playing small with your life?

Truth be told, many people are. Whether it's an addiction to mediocrity or a fear of failing, too many people live life in the small-to-medium range. And it's acceptable.

So, how do you know what kind of life you are capable of living? You try …

REFLECT AND GROW

1. Why might some people settle for playing small?

   _____

   _____

   _____

2. What is the cost of playing small?

   _____

   _____

   _____

   _____

Are You Hearing Multiple Voices?

When faced with a decision, do you hear multiple voices? If not, you should be ...

"The way of a fool is right in his own eyes, but a wise man listens to advice." – Proverbs 12:15

A fool hears one voice: his own. If someone disagrees with a fool, the other voice must be wrong — because the fool is always right in his own eyes.

Wise people, on the other hand, listen to other voices. You don't to agree with them; just listen to them. Every once and a while (or more often than that), we see that the other voice is right.

How many voices are you hearing?

Reflect and Grow

1. What keeps people from asking for help?

   _____

   _____

   _____

   _____

2. Which one are you most susceptible to?

   _____

   _____

   _____

   _____

   _____

   _____

3. Who are the wise people in your life?

   _____

   _____

   _____

   _____

   _____

   _____

Is Your Life A Candle Or A Torch

"Life is no brief candle to me. It is a sort of splendid torch which I've got ahold of for the moment, and I want to make it burn as brightly as possible before handing it on to future generations." – George Bernard Shaw

I first read this quote in Bob Buford's book "Halftime." Buford raises the all-important question: What are you doing with your life? More specifically, what will you do with the second half of life — should the good Lord give you a full four quarters?

Will you go through life carrying a candle or a torch? Will you flicker or beam brightly? Will you put off just enough light to crack the darkness or chase the darkness or away?

Thirteen years ago I decided to be a torch. Rather, God called me to be a torch. Through a season of searching and prayer, God placed three things on my heart that were to be my life's narrative from that point forward: start new churches, reach my generation for Jesus, and train the next generation of church leaders.

That torch has lit the way for tremendous change in my life. At times it has felt too hot to handle. Torches are like that.

Yet, in the words of Neil Young, "it's better to burn out than it is to rust."

I don't want rust. I want my torch to "burn as brightly as possible."

How about you? Candle or torch?

REFLECT AND GROW

1. Which would you rather be, a brief candle or a splendid torch?

   _____

   _____

   _____

   _____

   _____

2. What is one thing you can do today to start burning bright?

   _____

   _____

   _____

   _____

   _____

THE BUCK STOPS HERE

It's true: I'm a news geek. I watch the news, read it on my phone, and even watch C-SPAN on occasion (and not just the free-for-all British Parliament programming).

Normally I don't venture into the political waters. And this particular post is not intended for political purposes. But something happened recently that I believe applies to leaders at all levels: Good leaders accept responsibility and accountability for what happens on their watch.

You probably know about the attack on the U.S. Embassy in Libya. Four people were killed, including an ambassador. The spin/fall-out/excuses started immediately. The first explanation blamed the deadly uproar on a YouTube video. Later we learned it wasn't a spontaneous attack, it had been planned for quite a while. Yet people kept appearing on news programs telling us it was the video's fault.

Then they started throwing each other (and each other's agencies) under the bus. "Nobody told us." "We didn't know." It's the _____ (fill-in your favorite politician or agency's name) fault.

Yesterday, Secretary of State Hillary Clinton threw herself under the bus: "I take responsibility."

President Harry Truman had a sign on his desk that read, "The buck stops here."

That doesn't mean Harry Truman (or any president or leader) must make every decision. It does mean that good leaders accept responsibility for those they lead. And with responsibility comes accountability.

Good leaders take the blame and spread the credit — that's why they inspire trust and confidence. Poor leaders spread the blame and take the credit — that's why no one wants to die on the hill with them.

Where does the buck stop with you?

REFLECT AND GROW

1. Would those you lead say you hold yourself accountable for your actions? Yes / No

2. How do you show accountability?

_____

_____

_____

_____

_____

_____

_____

Peace And Thankfulness

"Let the peace of Christ rule in your hearts, since as members of one body you were called to peace. And be thankful." – Colossians 3:15

I read this verse this morning and thought about the connection between peace and thankfulness. It's there. It's definitely there.

The most peaceful people I know tend to be the most thankful people I know.

There is a gratitude that flows from them in every conversation, in every situation. You can't talk with them long before hearing words like "blest," "fortunate," "grateful" and others like that.

Conflict is fueled by a sense of being wronged. It is fostered when one person feels cheated or deprived of something.

Contentment, on the other hand, flows out of thankfulness. And content people tend to be peaceful people. If I am content, I do not have to resent you for what you have and what I don't have. My contentment is internal.

The next time you are feeling anxious, fearful, or just plain contentious … ask yourself this question:

"What do I have to be thankful for?"

Peace be with you.

REFLECT AND GROW

1. List five things that you are thankful today:

   _____

   _____

   _____

   _____

   _____

   _____

   _____

   _____

   _____

   _____

What Are You Working Towards

Many years ago Stephen Covey wrote the best-selling book, "Seven Habits of Highly Effective People." One of those habits was: "Begin with the end in mind." In other words, define what you're working towards before you start.

On paper, this seems to make sense. Before you get in the car, know where you are going.
But in many ways, we hop in the car and try to figure out as we're driving where it is we are going.

- In your career, what does success look like?
- If you're a Christ-follower, what does a mature Christ-follower look like?
- If you're a youth pastor, what do you want a graduating senior to be like? To know?
- If you're married, what does a healthy, fulfilling marriage look like?
- If you're a pastor, what does a growing church look like?

Once the end is defined, the steps to get there usually fall in place. In order to get to the store, I know where I need to turn.

The other option is to get in the car and just start driving. We may or may not find the right path. We might be lost and not know it. It will take longer to get there, if we get there at all. Or even worse, we might be lost and think we are where we are supposed to be.

Spending a few minutes (or days) defining the end will not only save time in the long run, it will save you a lot of headaches and heart aches.

So, what are you working towards?

REFLECT AND GROW

1. Do you have a sense of destiny? Yes / No

2. In your most relationship, what does success look like?

_____

_____

_____

_____

_____

_____

_____

_____

_____

Difficulties And Determination

This past weekend, I spoke on the early church and their response to opposition. Instead of praying for deliverance, they prayed for boldness: **"Now, Lord, consider their threats and enable your servants to speak your word with great boldness"** (Acts 4:29).

Let's be honest: Most of us would have prayed for deliverance. "God, get rid of these people ... fix this problem ... smooth out this bump ... give me more money!" Instead, these believers prayed for a boldness equal to their challenge.

Here's the choice we must make when faced with difficulties: Will I allow these difficulties to <u>deepen</u> my determination or <u>defeat</u> my determination?

Often, we allow difficulties to defeat our determination. Or, to put it this way, we give up. We walk away, give in, fold over. Is there a proper time to quit? Yes. Sometimes it is foolish to continue down an unproductive path.

However, just as often, we quit too soon. We stop short of receiving our second wind. We sit when we could have pushed a little further.

Here's the key: Difficulties will deepen your determination when you really, really believe in what you're fighting for.

If you believe in it, then dig in. Put down a stake. Take a stand. Let every difficulty be an opportunity to reaffirm your commitment.

REFLECT AND GROW

1. Have you ever given up too soon? If so, what caused you to give up?

   _____

   _____

   _____

   _____

   _____

2. List one thing you have (or want to have) that is worth fighting for:

   _____

   _____

   _____

   _____

   _____

BEYOND TEAMWORK

One of my favorite sermon series I did while planting LifePoint was one that examined the leadership of Moses. We took about six weeks and looked at the various aspects of his leadership, from his calling to how he handled challenges.

Numbers 11 is a good example. The burden of leading a surly group like the Israelites was taking its toll on Moses. The chapter begins with the people complaining (no surprise there). Scholars estimate the number of people Moses was leading to be between 500,000 and a million. That's no small number.

Moses is ready to walk away. The loneliness of leadership is almost too much.

That's when God offers a remedy. It's found in Numbers 11:16-17 ... *"The Lord said to Moses: 'Bring me seventy of Israel's elders **who are known to you** as leaders and officials among the people. Have them come to the Tent of Meeting, that they may stand there with you. I will come down and speak with you there, and **I will take of the Spirit that is on you and put the Spirit on them**. They will help you carry the burden of the people so that you will not have to carry it alone'"* (emphasis mine).

Two things stand out.

First, Moses was not to select random people to help share the load. There would be no lottery system. These were to be men who were known to Moses as ones who were leaders. Since they would be working closely with Moses, it was important for them to have a relationship with him.

The second thing is what God promised to do: put the Spirit that is in Moses in the men Moses selected. God is longing to reproduce good leaders. We certainly participate in that reproduction through mentoring, coaching, and discipling up-and-coming leaders. In the end, however, it is God who will put his Spirit in those that he has chosen.

This is how God moves his people beyond teamwork to true community.

REFLECT AND GROW

1. In your own words, describe the difference between teamwork and community:

   _____

   _____

   _____

   _____

   _____

   _____

   _____

   _____

Do You Have A Different Spirit

Numbers 14 is a great chapter in the Old Testament, not so much for how it starts. The chapter begins with the Israelites grumbling and complaining:

That night all the members of the community raised their voices and wept aloud. All the Israelites grumbled against Moses and Aaron, and the whole assembly said to them, "If only we had died in Egypt! Or in this wilderness! Why is the Lord bringing us to this land only to let us fall by the sword? Our wives and children will be taken as plunder. Wouldn't it be better for us to go back to Egypt?" And they said to each other, "We should choose a leader and go back to Egypt." -- (Numbers 14:1-4)

Listening to their complaints, one might have thought they had left behind the lifestyle of the rich and famous. To hear them speak, life in Egypt was life on easy street. It's remarkable how easily our memory fails us.

Truth be told, they had been slaves in Egypt. No freedom. No independence. Life had been hard. Really hard. And now they're clamoring to go back.

This doesn't sit too well with God: *"I will strike them down with a plague and destroy them ..."* (Numbers 14:12). I'm reading between the lines here, but I think God doesn't like grumbling and complaining all that much.

Fortunately for the Israelites, Moses pleads their case and God relents. Plague avoided. Even though he relents, he's still not too happy with them. With one exception — Caleb. Remember him? One of the 12 spies who snuck into the Promise Land. Along with Joshua, he was the only other spy who actually thought the Israelites could take the land. The other 10 lacked the faith and courage to recommend fighting.

Listen to what God says about Caleb:

*"But because my servant Caleb **has a different spirit and follows me wholeheartedly**, I will bring him into the land he went to, and his descendants will inherit it"* (Numbers 14:24, emphasis mine).

What is the difference between those who grumble and complain and get nowhere and those who advance and take the land? Two things:

1. A different spirit (or way of looking at life)

2. Complete obedience (a willingness to follow God wholeheartedly)

It starts with seeing and ends with following.

Leaders, teachers, parents, coaches — do you have a different spirit? Faithful leaders will always have a slightly different spirit than those they lead. That's the nature of faith. It sees things others cannot (or choose not to) see.

REFLECT AND GROW

1. Of all the leaders you know, which of them has a "different" spirit?

_____

_____

_____

_____

_____

2. How can you begin to see the people you lead, your circumstances, even your problems differently?

_____

_____

_____

_____

_____

Are You Guarding Your Deposit

"Guard the good deposit that was entrusted to you — guard it with the help of the Holy Spirit who lives in us" -- 2 Timothy 1:14

As I grow older, I'm more drawn to the idea of stewardship ... being a good steward of all that God has entrusted to me. This includes finances but is so much more than that. It also includes my family, time, talents, dreams, and influence.

Paul tells Timothy to "guard the good deposit that was entrusted" to him. Have you ever thought of your talents as God's deposit in your life? God invested in you. Your abilities are not your own. God gave them to you.

To be a good steward of the resources entrusted to me, I must guard them. This does not mean hiding them. I do not honor God by refusing to share what he has entrusted to me. I honor him when I refine, increase, and expand what he has deposited with me. Since I believe God gave me the gift of teaching, I'm continually trying to get better. Why? I am responsible for what I do with what God has given me.

Fortunately, we are not in this life alone. Paul reminds Timothy that the Holy Spirit is there to help him. God wants you to succeed even more than you want yourself to succeed. It is his name and reputation that is on the line.

Are you guarding what God has entrusted to you?

REFLECT AND GROW

1. How would you define stewardship?

   _____

   _____

   _____

   _____

   _____

2. What leadership qualities have been entrusted to you?

   _____

   _____

   _____

   _____

   _____

Calling Forth Potential

"For this reason I remind you to fan into flame the gift of God, which is in you through the laying on of my hands. For the Spirit God gave us does not make us timid, but gives us power, love and self-discipline" -- 2 Timothy 2:6-7

I read that passage yesterday afternoon, surrounded by towering redwood trees. I had hiked up the prayer trail at Opportunity Camp, settling in on a bench that provided a great view of the trees (especially when lying flat on your back).

My thoughts and prayers drifted to the kids who were then enjoying open recreation time. I wondered how many of them had someone who spoke into their life the way that Paul spoke into the life of Timothy — because he believed in Timothy.

Too often, those who speak into our lives do not speak the truth into our lives but lies. They tear down rather than build up. Back home, many of these kids at camp experience this on a daily basis. They get told how bad they are, how worthless they are. Rather than be given aspirations, they get desperation.

I was blessed to be raised by parents who believed in me and told me so. My mother sent me a birthday card while I was in college that called forth my potential in her simple but direct way: you have the world by the tail and can swing it any way you want to.

I was also blessed to have a minister-mentor who took an awkward high school student by his side and told me he saw leadership in me.

What is the greatest gift you can give a young person? It might be to simply recognize that they have a gift and then to tell them about it. The difference between a life of mediocrity and a life of effectiveness may be the presence of someone who believes in them. It may take you believing in them before they will believe in themselves.

What may seem like a casual comment to you may be life-changing for them.

REFLECT AND GROW

1. Who identified potential in you?

   _____

   _____

   _____

   _____

2. Who needs to hear encouragement from you?

   _____

   _____

   _____

   _____

Investing In Shade Trees

Elton Trueblood was a Quaker and a theologian. He spent most of his career working on a college campus, at places such as Harvard and Stanford. Being surrounded by college students, it's not surprising he once wrote: *"A man has made at least a start on discovering the meaning of human life when he plants shade trees under which he knows full well he never will sit."*

In a world that is increasingly about instant gratification and getting our way, Trueblood's words are a good reminder that God calls us to think forward.

The apostle Paul would put it this way: *"And the things you have heard me say in the presence of many witnesses entrust to reliable men who will also be qualified to teach others"* (2 Timothy 2:2).

It is a sign of maturity to invest in others without expecting an immediate return. The formation process takes time. Some lessons can be taught but must be internalized through experience.

Within the church, are we investing in the shade trees of tomorrow? How many churches have an active, intentional way of encouraging young people to consider full-time ministry as a vocation?

When I was in high school, Brad Carman (our local preacher) invested in a young sapling, believing that I had the potential to become a shade tree in the future.

There are several young guys on our staff and in our church that I try to spend time with — no agenda or curriculum. Just face-to-face time. I'm there to hear what they dream about, struggle with, and hope to become. I believe they have the potential to become shade trees.

A faithful and faith-filled church will invest dollars, time, and energy into the leaders of tomorrow. While we may benefit from the growth of their branches as they learn and develop, the majority of their influence may come at a later date, in another place.

I'm OK with that.

REFLECT AND GROW

1. What shade trees are you planting?

   _____

   _____

   _____

   _____

   _____

   _____

   _____

   _____

Guarding Your Heart

When I went through church planting boot camp* with Stadia, I was given a plaque with my name on one side and these words inscribed on the back: ***"Above all else, guard your heart, for it is the wellspring of life"*** (Proverbs 4:23).

It was a reminder to those of us who were about to start a new church that perhaps the most difficult thing we would do would not be finding launch team members or a facility. It would be to guard our heart. To not become overly inflated or unduly depressed. To not become prideful or pitiful.

That verse came back to me this morning in my devotional time. It wasn't written just for church planters or even pastors. It was written to everybody who wants to live a life that honors God and pleases him. Simply put, it's good medicine. For when a person doesn't guard their heart, they leave it exposed to all sorts of attacks, from within and without.

Guarding your heart is not the same as walling it off and hiding it away. A hidden heart is not a guarded heart.

Guarding your heart is about checking your motives, ensuring that you are not reacting defensively when the proper response would be humility. It's also about not tolerating behaviors or influences that diminish you — both your own behavior and that of others. Only so much water can roll off a duck's back before the duck drowns.

Here are a few things I do to ensure I'm guarding my heart as best as I can:

- I routinely pray and ask God to reveal "any offensive way in me, and lead me in the way everlasting" (Psalm 139:24). I need to know if I am out-of-bounds.

- I ask those I trust if I came across in a tense conversation or discussion as defensive or accusatory. Many times they provide me with beneficial counsel.

- I try to surround myself with more positive influences than negative ones. Surrounding yourself with people of questionable character or integrity will challenge your heart.

- I read as much as I can. The Bible is the best source for learning how to react, protect, and deflect. After the Bible, I try to fill my mind with good information and ideas from all kinds of sources.

- I try not to lower myself to the level of those who do not hold themselves to higher standards. If a person lies to you, it does not justify lying to them in return.

Why does it matter how well you guard your heart? The Bible answers that question: the heart is the "wellspring of life." Lose your heart, lose your life. It's that important.

REFLECT AND GROW

1. What are you praying for in this season of life?

   _____

   _____

_____

_____

2. Who are the positive influences in your life?

_____

_____

_____

_____

3. What are you reading?

_____

_____

_____

_____

_____

_____

BOSS OR LEADER

"A boss creates fear; a leader confidence. A boss fixes blame; a leader corrects mistakes. A boss knows all; a leader asks questions." – Russell H. Ewing

Ewing raises a good distinction between being a boss and being a leader. This applies just as much in the family as it does in the workplace. Do you boss your children or lead them? Do you boss your employees or lead them?

Both approaches may work — but only for a little while. No one likes to be bossed around. But do people like to be lead? If you distinguish between bossing and leading, I would answer, "Yes." People like to be lead by those who develop their talents, care about their dreams, and are generous with appreciation.

At home or work, are you more concerned with being followed than you are about leading? Are you more comfortable being a boss because leading requires giving up control? Are you seeking to retain power (boss) or do you seek to empower those around you?

Truth is, you have a choice. Choose wisely.

REFLECT AND GROW

1. Are you more of a boss or leader?

   _____

   _____

   _____

2. What is one boss-like action you can stop doing?

_____
_____
_____
_____
_____
_____
_____
_____
_____
_____
_____
_____

What Are You Pursuing

"There are many things in life that will catch your eye, but only a few that will catch your heart. Pursue those." — Anonymous

Truth be told, we humans are easily distracted by the shiny things in life. We drift towards those things that catch our eye. We spend the better part of our days, the best of our energy, in pursuit of more ... money or stuff or gadgets.

What if you spent the better part of your day, the best of your energy, pursuing the one or two things that have captivated your heart?

Imagine how your day, your family, your job, and your community would be different.

Reflect and Grow

1. What are you easily distracted by and why?

   _____

   _____

   _____

   _____

   _____

2. What captures your heart?

_____
_____
_____
_____
_____
_____
_____
_____
_____
_____
_____
_____
_____
_____

GOOD LEADERS INSPIRE

John Quincy Adams, the sixth President of the United States, once defined leadership in these terms: ***"If your actions inspire others to dream more, learn more, do more and become more, you are a leader."***

That's a great definition. You've probably heard that leadership is influence (thanks to John Maxwell). That's true. If you're not influencing someone, you're not leading them. Take Maxwell's definition and through it in the blender with President Adam's definition — and you have a really good definition of leadership.

Ask yourself the following questions ...

- Do the people I lead dream bigger dreams than before?
- Do the people I lead show a desire to learn more than before?
- Do the people I lead do more on their own initiative, without my prompting?
- Do the people I lead become better leaders?

Here's why many leaders will struggle with these questions: for them, leadership isn't about those they lead — it's about themselves. Production-oriented leaders may still have influence (and by definition still be a leader), but they may be failing to harness the power of inspiration.

The power of inspiration enables a team to go further than a production-mindset allows. Teams that are dreaming more, learning more, doing more, and becoming more will accomplish more.

Adams' definition of leadership applies across many landscapes. Parenting, coaching, pastoring, managing, mentoring.

If you applied the four questions above to your key relationships, how would they change?

REFLECT AND GROW

1. Using Adams' definition of leadership, how are you doing?

   _____

   _____

   _____

   _____

   _____

   _____

   _____

Black Holes

A black hole is a *"region of space-time where gravity is so strong that nothing that enters the region, not even light, can escape"* (Wikipedia).

Black holes are the enemies of good ideas.

A father can become a black hole if he puts down every suggestion. Children want to be affirmed, to feel valued. No one wants to be constantly put-down. The easiest way to avoid a put-down? Offer no suggestions.

A boss can become a black hole if he or she believes every good idea must originate with them. Employees who offer ideas only to see them dry up or go unused will eventually stop offering ideas.

A friend can become a black hole if they treat opinions with sarcasm. Not every opinion is equal. Not every opinion is correct. But every opinion is personal, even the most hair-brained idea. Sarcasm communicates a lack of appreciation — not just for the opinion, but for the person.

A black hole is anything that shuts down the production of good ideas. The question for any leader, father, or friend is this: am I creating the kind of environment where good ideas go to die?

Reflect and Grow

1. What behaviors or attitudes create black holes?

_____

_____

_____

_____

_____

_____

_____

2. What can you do to become more receptive to the ideas of others?

_____

_____

_____

_____

_____

_____

_____

INFLUENCE AND INFLUENZA

"The words influence and influenza are cousins." — David Jeremiah

We are a contagious people and not just when it comes to germs and viruses and hand sanitizer.

Attitudes are contagious. One sour person can sink an entire meeting. A little grumpiness goes a long way. On the other hand, a gentle answer to a harsh question can soften the atmosphere (that should be in the Bible!).

Vision is contagious. I believe people are hungry for a higher purpose than Angry Birds or voting on American Idol. A clearly articulated, passionate vision will spread — hopping from one carrier to another.

Morals (or lack of) are contagious. Parents understand this. It's why we pray for our children to make good friends, to surround themselves with positive influences. But what about at work? When a leader lacks a moral compass, the moral temperature gets set at whatever degree is in the room and it is usually the lowest common denominator. When you refuse to bend or twist or cut a corner, that sense of integrity becomes contagious.

Generosity is contagious. So is compassion. As well as kindness.

What else have you caught lately?

REFLECT AND GROW

1. How contagious are you in terms of …

   Attitude:

   _____

   _____

   _____

   _____

   Vision:

   _____

   _____

   _____

   _____

   Morals:

   _____

   _____

   _____

   _____

Displacement

Thanks to his bathtub, Archimedes discovered the concept of displacement. As he sat down in his bathtub, he noticed the water level would rise. The weight of his body displaced the water. From this epiphany, he realized he could use similar experiments to measure the volume of certain objects.

In life, we have ...

- **Placements:** things that are in their proper place.
- **Misplacements:** things that are not placed in their proper place
- **Displacements:** things that are replaced by other things.

Displacement shows up when we transfer our feelings about one thing/person/situation to another thing/person/situation. In counseling terms, it's called "kicking the dog." You "kick the dog" when, after a hard day at work, you come home and kick the dog. The dog didn't cause your bad day — you simply displaced your frustration.

Often times, we practice displacement and don't even know it. Little things that might not otherwise bother us become big explosions. Or, we transfer the intensity of our disappointment in one area to a minor infraction in another.

Displacement is not inevitable ... unless you're taking a bath.

REFLECT AND GROW

1. Do you have a tendency to practice displacement?

   _____

   _____

   _____

   _____

2. How can you guard against practicing displacement?

   _____

   _____

   _____

   _____

   _____

   _____

   _____

FOR OR WITH

Perry Noble says the number one sign of an insecure leader is that they see people as working <u>for</u> them and not <u>with</u> them.

These two small words (a combined seven letters, average of 3.5 letters per word) reflect a large difference in attitude. This difference not only affects the leader's style but how the people respond to their leadership.

I've told my children, "There's a difference between 'I've <u>got</u> to do something' and 'I <u>get</u> to do something.'"

When you've <u>got</u> to do something, it's often viewed as a burden. You do it because you are obligated or fearful of what will happen if you don't do it.

When you <u>get</u> to do something, it's act of passion or purpose. You don't watch the clock or groan about it.

As a leader, if you view people as working for you it is likely they will perceive their tasks as things they've got to do. Why? Because they have <u>got</u> to do this <u>for</u> you.

If you see people as working with you, it's likely you will spend the time to learn what motivates them. You will have them saying, "I get to do this."

What do you think?

REFLECT AND GROW

1. Describe the difference between working for someone and working with them:

_____

_____

_____

_____

_____

_____

2. Do you have people working for you or with you?

_____

_____

_____

_____

_____

_____

_____

Telling Stories

As a young preacher, I learned one important truth: people will forget your main points but they will remember your stories. In fact, I've become convinced that I could preach the same points multiple times and people wouldn't notice — but tell the same story and it's immediately familiar!

That's the power of a story. Are you harnessing the power of stories?

If you are a communicator, stories are your best friend. They take your main point from gray scale to full color. Stories do more than fill space: they motivate, inspire, challenge, and create memories that become portable. A well-told story is a gift to your listeners. It allows them to say in a different time and place, "That reminds me of a story."

If you are a leader, stories become the glue that holds a vision together. "Do you remember when …" is the beginning of a story that reminds teammates of a time when the vision came alive, was threatened, or moved forward. Good leaders are good story tellers. And here's the good thing: you don't have to create the stories. Many of the best stories come directly from the front lines. Your job is to gather and retell them.

If you are a parent, family stories are what create a sense of belonging, a sense of rootedness. Stories reinforce family values. While you could sit them down on the couch and lecture them about work ethic (good luck with that), a story about grandpa might serve you better.

Everyone loves a good story.

REFLECT AND GROW

1. What are the components of a good story?

   _____

   _____

   _____

   _____

   _____

   _____

   _____

   _____

   _____

   _____

   _____

   _____

   _____

Your Personal Battery

Have you ever licked a battery to see if it still had any juice in it? Me neither.

In the days before rechargeable batteries, when a battery went dead you would throw it away. Now you just plug in your iPod or phone (or car) and recharge the battery. It's a wonderful thing!

When it comes to your personal battery, there are two important questions to ask: What drains my battery? and What recharges my battery?

It may be that what drains your battery is unavoidable — life happens. We have responsibilities that must be lived up to. It takes effort to be productive.

On the other hand, some of what drains our batteries might be unnecessary. Distinguishing the necessary from the unnecessary — and reducing the unnecessary — actually extends our battery life.

How do you recharge your battery? Do you read? Exercise? Take a day trip? Have a 5 Hour Energy Drink? It will be different for each person. In fact, what may recharge your battery may actually drain mine.

Most of us never fully recharge our battery; we plug in long enough to get through the afternoon or meeting or weekend. Eventually, this catches up to us and the battery may no longer hold a full charge.

So ... what drains your battery? How do you recharge?

REFLECT AND GROW

1. What drains your battery?

   _____

   _____

   _____

   _____

   _____

2. What recharges your battery?

   _____

   _____

   _____

   _____

   _____

   _____

Why Good Leaders Are Good Communicators

"For a leader, communication is connection and inspiration – not just transmission of information." – Gary Burnison, The Twelve Absolutes of Leadership

Most of may remember the basic definition of communication we learned in school: you have a sender and a receiver and information flows between the two. Communication has occurred if the transmission was successful.

Along the way, we recognize the deficiencies in such a definition. If the receiver doesn't understand what the sender has said, no matter how often he or she says it, communication has not occurred. If the sender isn't listening, communication has not occurred. And, according to Gary Burnison, if the transmission of information is the only goal, communication has not occurred.

Good leaders understand that one role of communication is to forge a connection with the listener. A good speech or conversation reinforces what the sender and receiver have in common. Leaders (or preachers or teachers) use communication moments as an opportunity to build bridges. A good preacher will speak to the pathos of the crowd, saying, "I am one of you."

Good leaders also recognize the inspiration aspect of communication. We all can sense the difference between one who talks because she likes to hear herself talk and the one who talks because she has our interest at heart. There are teachers who are only concerned with transmitting facts; and then there are teachers who hope to instill a passion for the subject within their students. Leaders from Jesus to Abraham Lincoln to Martin Luther King, Jr., have seized communication moments and turned them into catalytic events.

Words can either inspire, deflate, or bore. Wise leaders choose them wisely.

REFLECT AND GROW

1. What are you doing to become a better communicator?

   _____

   _____

   _____

   _____

   _____

   _____

   _____

Living In The Sweet Spot

Tennis rackets have them. So do baseball bats. On any given swing, you know when you get it right ... and when you don't.

I'm talking about the sweet spot — that place on the racket or bat that produces the best result. Hit it there and the ball takes off; miss by a few inches and you have a squibber (that's baseball talk for a weak hit).

God has wired each of us with our own unique sweet spot. It's a mix of gifts, abilities, talents, and experiences. The sweet spot may show up on the job or in areas we love to volunteer in.

When we're operating in our sweet spot, time either stands still or flies by. Athletes call this being in the "zone." Operating in our sweet spot energizes us and those around us. When we're outside of our sweet spot, it drains us (and, if we're honest, it probably drains those around us, too).

Not every minute of every day will be spent in your sweet spot. But if a significant portion of your week is spent on the outer edges, it will eventually catch up to you.

There are great tools for discovering your sweet spot: SHAPE tests and Strengths Finder are two that I have used. Feedback from people you trust and respect helps as well.

Discover your sweet spot and try to live in it as much as possible.

REFLECT AND GROW

1. How would you define your sweet spot?

   _____
   _____
   _____
   _____
   _____
   _____
   _____

2. What percentage of the time do you operate in your sweet spot?

   _____
   _____
   _____
   _____

Are You A Contributor Or Consumer?

We are a nation of consumers. Where I went to college, a town of only 3,000 people, there were more restaurants than places to get your hair cut. Surprisingly, no enterprising entrepreneur ever combined the two.

We consume ... food, toys, gadgets, data, information, internet, news, entertainment ... in short, we consume everything.

Just this morning, I consumed bacon, eggs, and coffee.

The problem is not with consumption per se* but when we develop a consumer mentality. What does a consumer mentality look like?

- When you ask, "What will you do for me?" before you ask, "What can I do for you?"
- When you would rather have your hand out than to offer a helping hand.
- When you process every decision through the filter of your own feelings instead of asking, "Is this the right thing to do?"

When the consumer mentality shows up at work, it creates a passive culture. When the consumer mentality shows up at church, it creates a selfish culture. When the consumer mentality shows up at home, it creates an argumentative culture.

Here's the good news: we have a choice. We can choose to approach life as a consumer, seeking only what's in it for us. Or, we can opt to become a contributor, looking for ways to create, add, and contribute to those around us.

The debate over consumer vs. contributor is not political; it is personal. It's more about your attitude than your aptitude.

What about you?

REFLECT AND GROW

1. What are the consumer symptoms to look for?

   _____

   _____

   _____

   _____

   _____

   _____

   _____

   _____

RISK

"The person who risks nothing, does nothing, has nothing, is nothing, and becomes nothing. He may avoid suffering and sorrow, but he simply cannot learn and feel and change and grow and love and live." – Leo Buscaglia

Buscaglia was right.

Risk is not only a part of life, it is one of life's best growth engines. When a child is no longer satisfied to scoot along the floor, she takes the risk of learning to walk. Without taking that risk, she would never learn to skip, hop, or run.

When we get to the dating and courtship phase of life, there is the risk she will say no.

Those who have started businesses or churches or organizations, understand the risk of failing comes with the territory.

Artists who take their craft from the basement to the stage, risk rejection.

As Buscaglia says, you may avoid suffering and sorrow but you also avoid satisfaction, too.

REFLECT AND GROW

1. Why do many people avoid any risk at all?

   _____

2. When a person avoids risk, what are they also giving up on?

Moving And Settling

The minute you stop moving, you start settling.

If you stop pursuing better communication with your spouse, you are settling for the level of discourse you have now.

If you stop reading books that stretch your mind, you are settling for the knowledge you have now.

If you stop exercising, you are settling for the health you have now.

If you stop pursuing your dreams, you are settling for your present achievements — soon to be past accomplishments.

Reflect and Grow

1. Why is it tempting to be a settler?

   _____

   _____

   _____

   _____

   _____

2. What is one thing you can do today to start moving in a specific area?

_____

_____

_____

_____

_____

_____

_____

_____

_____

_____

_____

_____

Authentic Living – What's Missing

Inevitably, once you've clarified your values and beliefs, you'll notice something: my behavior doesn't always match my beliefs.

For example, I might say I value family but if my schedule shows I'm hardly ever home, there is a gap between what I believe and how I behave. In order to live authentically, something must change — either my beliefs or my behavior.

If I'm unwilling to change my belief because I feel it is non-negotiable, then my behavior must change.

How does a person live with authenticity? For starters, it begins with clarity in terms of what you believe. What are your values? Convictions? Non-negotiables? Authenticity means being true to the real you.

Once you've clarified your beliefs and values, ask yourself this question: Does my behavior match my beliefs?

Reflect and Grow

1. List one or two beliefs you hold as non-negotiable?

   _____

   _____

2. Is there a behavior you need to change to bring it into alignment with one of those beliefs?

Insecurity Minimizes Potential

Over the last few days I've been watching online training videos from the Association of Related Churches. ARC exists to help start churches that start churches. The training videos feature Chris Hodges, senior pastor at The Church of the Highlands.

Yesterday I watched a video entitled, "Teamwork Makes the Dream Work." At the end, the late Billy Hornsby spoke for a few minutes and said this: "You cannot be insecure and build great teams."

That one line was worth the entire video.

Effective leaders are not perfect nor superhuman. In fact, effective leaders know their strengths AND their weaknesses. Being secure in their strengths, they know better than trying to operate in areas of weaknesses.

When a leader is insecure, it shows up in many different ways.

- Insecure leaders hold too tightly to things they should let go of.
- Insecure leaders have more answers than they do questions.
- Insecure leaders will persist in a wrong direction rather than admitting failure.
- Insecure leaders will lash out at those they perceive to be more secure.

- Insecure leaders lead from moods rather than convictions.
- Insecure leaders find it hard to rejoice in the success of others.

This principle applies to families, classrooms, board rooms, as well as in the church.

What has been your experience?

REFLECT AND GROW

1. What causes a person to feel insecure?

   _____
   _____
   _____
   _____
   _____
   _____
   _____
   _____

Do What You Love

When it comes to work or vocation, it's common to hear people say: "Do what you love." Sounds good ...

But I love eating donuts. As much as I love donuts, I know if I only eat donuts, I'll die a fat (but happy) man. To be healthy, I can't just eat what I love — sometimes I have to eat things that I know are good for me but may not be the most enjoyable experience.

Successful people don't just do what they love (i.e., are passionate about); they also do what they are good at. They take into account their strengths and act accordingly. Satisfaction comes when passion and strengths are aligned.

What do you love? Are you good at it? Getting better?

Reflect and Grow

1. If you could draft a dream job description, what would it be?

   _____
   _____
   _____
   _____

Metabolizing A Situation

This morning I finished reading Henry Cloud's book "Necessary Endings." Let me rephrase that: I came to the end of the book this morning and I'm already re-reading it. Some books are like that.

One of the last concepts he talks about in the book is the idea of metabolizing a situation, experience, or outcome.

The idea is simple. In physical terms, our bodies take in two types of foods: useful and wasteful. Useful food gets digested and put to work. Wasteful foods get processed and left behind. While the thought of creating a more graphic visual is enticing, I will leave it at that.

- Healthy people metabolize well.
- Healthy organizations metabolize well.
- Healthy relationships metabolize well.

The problem is ... outside of the physical manifestation of metabolism, most of us never do it. We experience a setback and don't take the time to dissect what went right and what went wrong. We experience a traumatic event and don't reflect on what we learned and what we hope to avoid in the future. We hit a home run and forget all the little pieces that went into a larger success.

In terms of negative experiences, a failure to properly metabolize a situation almost always puts us on the track of repeating it in the future.

How is your metabolism?

REFLECT AND GROW

1. Describe your most recent leadership success?

   _____
   _____
   _____
   _____
   _____
   _____
   _____

2. Why do you think it was successful?

   _____
   _____
   _____
   _____
   _____
   _____
   _____

Setup For Success

Our daughters are on their way to Sol Vista ski basin to take their first snowboarding lessons. I'm excited for them ... they are young and resilient enough to learn the right way now and then enjoy it for years to come.

The same is true whether it's learning to golf or play the piano. If you can master the fundamentals at an early age, you'll set yourself up for a life of enjoyment and improvement.

The same is true in life.

In a marriage, you set yourself up for success by learning to communicate effectively and handle conflict honestly. The sooner you do so, the better.

In coaching a team, you set yourself up for success by practice, practice, practice. But not just busywork; practicing the right way to do it, every time.

In leadership, you set yourself up for success by elevating the abilities of those around you.

Getting setup for success is not the same as succeeding. But it's often hard to succeed when you haven't prepared the way ahead of time.

Reflect and Grow

1. What are the fundamentals when it comes to your specific job or role?

Refocus, Recalibrate, Renew

When it comes to celebrating New Year's Eve, I tend to follow the example of my dad: the best way to start the new year is with a good night's sleep. I don't believe there is anything magical about turning over a new calendar.

That being said, I do believe that each new year is a great time to refocus, recalibrate, and renew. In our culture, we rarely set aside time for reflection. We rush. We hurry. The business of introspection gets lost in the busyness of life.

Will you spend a few moments, minutes, or hours refining your focus? Life is too short to live aimlessly. Without a clear sense of purpose, we surrender our effectiveness to the circumstances that surround us. Is that the best stewardship we can offer God?

Will you also find time to recalibrate? If you're like me, you've probably recognized a fair amount of drifting in your life. Are you living in alignment with your mission, vision, and purpose? Do your actions reflect your values? Are your words and deeds in harmony with one another? Drifting often happens incrementally but the danger can be exponential.

At the start of a new year, will you set aside time to renew? For many of us, Thanksgiving through the end of the year feels like a sprint. When our batteries are low, our abilities are low. We find ourselves taking shortcuts rather than doing the hard stuff that may be required. It becomes easier to download someone else's hard work than to do our own. Eventually, if we're not careful, the lack of renewal will lead to burn out.

Whether this happens in late December, early January, or the middle of summer — it doesn't matter when; it just matters that you do it.

REFLECT AND GROW

1. What do you need refocus on?

   _____

   _____

   _____

   _____

   _____

2. In your life, what needs to be recalibrated?

   _____

   _____

   _____

   _____

WHITE SPACE

Do you have enough white space in your life?

If you're like most people, the paper of life gets filled up with stuff. Things to do, appointments, and outright clutter. We're rushing from this place to that one. Even the margins of life have scribbles in them.

The symptoms of too little white space include:

- Little-to-no down time.
- Uncomfortableness with silence.
- A feeling of always being distracted.
- Feeling rushed.
- Feeling guilty if you're not doing something.

How do you recapture lost white space?

REFLECT AND GROW

1. How much margin do you have in your current schedule?

   _____

   _____

   _____

   _____

2. If you are low on white space, what will you do to create more?

_____

_____

_____

_____

_____

_____

_____

_____

_____

_____

_____

_____

Very Draining People

Gordon MacDonald once wrote about VDP's or Very Draining People. These are the people who drain our energy rather than refueling us. Into every life at least one VDP must wander. But we can choose to limit our exposure or interaction with them.

We can also choose to surround ourselves with more positive people. I love to be around believers and dreamers. These are the people who provide a mental pick-me-up when I need it.

Which are you?

Reflect and Grow

1. What actions or attitudes of others drain you?

   _____

   _____

   _____

   _____

   _____

2. What is one thing you can do to inspire rather than drain others?

_____
_____
_____
_____
_____
_____
_____
_____
_____
_____
_____
_____
_____

The Perspective Of Motivation

Staying motivated is easy when you love what you're doing. How do you stay motivated when you have to slog through the tedious parts of the day?

Well, it depends on your perspective.

In other words, how are you choosing to "see" what you're doing? Seeing something as tedious only makes it more tedious. As Victor Frankl wrote years ago, life and circumstances can take away every freedom but one: the freedom to choose your attitude.

Reflect and Grow

1. What keeps you motivated when the circumstances are difficult?

   _____

   _____

   _____

   _____

   _____

2. What is one negative attitude that you are choosing to have or hold?

_____

_____

_____

_____

_____

_____

_____

_____

_____

_____

_____

The Boys Will Be Home For Christmas

On December 17, 1903, after many attempts, the Wright brothers were successful in getting their "flying machine" off the ground.

They immediately telegraphed their sister, Katherine, with this message: "We have actually flown 120 feet. We will be home for Christmas." Katherine hurried to the editor of the local newspaper with the exciting news.

He took the telegram and responded, "How nice. The boys will be home for Christmas."

Amazingly, he totally missed the fact they had actually flown 120 feet!

It's possible to be so caught up in the ordinary tasks of the day that we completely miss those amazing moments around us.

Reflect and Grow

1. What is the most amazing thing you have witnessed recently?

   _____

   _____

   _____

2. What made it amazing?

Kingdom Networking

One of the things I enjoyed the most about living in the Bay Area in the late 90's was the energy of the tech industry. There were start-ups springing up everywhere. You'd meet guys at Starbucks (or Peet's!) who were writing their business plan on the back of a napkin.

When I ventured into that world in 1999, I found myself attending networking events in San Francisco with other young guys looking to strike a deal, get a job, or just enjoy the food. Lots of free food. The idea was simple: you walk up to someone, introduce yourself, and ask what they did. Within a few minutes you knew if you needed to talk more or bow out gracefully and move to the next person.

One of the values I hold to as a pastor involves networking — something I call "kingdom networking." Having grown up in a fellowship that kept to itself, we didn't take advantage of what other denominations had to offer. As I've grown older, I've discovered I have much to learn from other groups.

Within the past week I have met with the following people:

- A seminary student trying to find his way from a Presbyterian background to a non-denominational setting.
- A young minister who is considering making a ministry change.

- A retired professor who serves at a United Methodist Church.
- A church planting director for an interdenominational group here in Denver.

I encourage our staff at Mountainview to be kingdom networkers as well. It's not difficult to seek out others who are involved in your ministry area and most of them will be glad you did.

Too often, ministry people get stuck in the loop that is their church. It's easy to do. It's where our office is and we go there everyday. We see the same people, talk about the same things. Kingdom networking allows you to broaden your perspective and even make a friend in the process.

Are you a kingdom networker?

REFLECT AND GROW

1. Who are you networking with?

   _____

   _____

   _____

   _____

   _____

Nimbleness

I have served most of my adult life in the non-profit sector, with a few forays into the marketplace. Non-profits face very real challenges: inadequate funding, old technology, a reliance on volunteers. With the great challenges come great blessings: a sense of purpose, making a difference, serving with passion.

One of the challenges that is common to most organizations (but I believe non-profits may feel to a greater degree) is a lack of nimbleness.

What does this mean? I'm referring to the ability to quickly adapt or adjust to a change in business climate, opportunity, or crisis. As organizations grow older and larger, thicker layers of red tape may develop. As an entrepreneurial organization, decisions are made quickly and changed quickly. In a bureaucratic organization, decisions may be made after the opportunity has passed.

Being nimble is not the same as being fickle. It's not about being trendy or gimmicky. In fact, some of the most nimble organizations are the least trendy.

Being nimble requires a clear, shared sense of the desired outcome — and the freedom to get there without sitting through endless meetings or focus groups.

Being nimble means mistakes will be made. The alternative? Be rigid, miss opportunities, and rob those around you of learning by doing.

Nimbleness does not mean no one is in charge; far from it. It means that leadership has clearly communicated the direction and holds people accountable for moving the right way.

Is your organization nimble?

REFLECT AND GROW

1. What does a nimble organization look like to you?

   _____

   _____

   _____

   _____

   _____

   _____

   _____

   _____

   _____

   _____

Where Ideas Die

How do leaders get the best ideas?

Years ago I learned that not all the best ideas originated with me. That was a humbling experience — and one that has paid many dividends throughout the intervening years.

If you lead a team of people at work, are you getting the best ideas on the table? More importantly, are you getting them into circulation?

I've learned through the years that there are guaranteed ways to dry up the well of ideas.

- If every idea must be your idea, you are drying up the well.
- If suggestions are criticized before analyzed, you are drying up the well.
- If who gets the credit is an issue, you are drying up the well.
- If it has to be done your way, you are drying up the well.
- If ideas are asked for but never used, you are drying up the well.

What happens when the well runs dry? Innovation stops. Fear creeps in. People lose interest. Your best people drift away.

Keep the well primed and the ideas will flow.

REFLECT AND GROW

1. How are you ensuring that you're receiving the best ideas available?

   _____
   _____
   _____
   _____
   _____
   _____
   _____
   _____
   _____
   _____
   _____

Passion Regained

Passion wanes in the absence of purpose.

This isn't to say that every detail of every day must be done in accordance with some larger purpose. If you can, that's great. There are things we must do simply because they must be done.

But if we operate for too long outside of our purpose, our passion will suffer.

God designed each of us to live for something larger than ourselves. Your purpose might be educating young children in a classroom. It might be feeding the hungry or working with battered women. When you discover what that purpose is, you know it. You feel it. And when you are doing tangible things towards the accomplishment of that purpose, it feeds your passion.

If you find yourself having a hard time getting motivated, that may be a warning sign to check if you are operating within your purpose.

Reflect and Grow

1. What are 5-7 words you would use to describe your purpose?

   _____

   _____

   _____

_____

_____

_____

_____

_____

2. What can you do to reconnect with your purpose?

_____

_____

_____

_____

_____

_____

_____

_____

_____

Preparing Your Horse

"The horse is made ready for the day of battle, but victory rests with the Lord." (Proverbs 21:31)

As a young pastor, I believed it was my responsibility to get the horse ready for battle AND to win the victory. That kind of thinking is the result of several things:

1. Stupidity
2. Immaturity
3. Arrogance

This is only one extreme. The other is to believe we don't have to do anything at all and can sit back and wait for God to act.

I've learned through the years that God expects me to act on things that are under my control. When possible, be prepared, be ready. It's why we must continue to learn, expanding our mental resources.

In the end, however, the outcome rests with God. He is not bound to my preparation (or lack of). Success in ministry, success in life, is in God's hands. That takes away a tremendous amount of pressure.

As you look at your responsibilities this upcoming week, are you doing a good job getting the horse ready for battle?

REFLECT AND GROW

1. In your organization, list a few things that are outside of your control:

   _____

   _____

   _____

   _____

   _____

2. List one thing you do have control over:

   _____

   _____

   _____

   _____

   _____

Comfort Or Cause

Back in the early 1990's, the church I was pastoring in San Diego sponsored a conference and brought in a friend of mine from Seattle. I had first met Milton Jones when one of my older brothers had interned with him at the Northwest Church in Seattle.

I don't remember sermon titles or stories, but I do remember one particularly passionate moment. Milt looked at the crowd and said, "What would you put up with in order to see someone come to Jesus?" Then he preceded to rattle off several things that our particular fellowship liked to hold dear. Would we give those up if it meant more people would find their way back to God?

It was an unsettling question for some in the crowd. The unspoken answer was likely "no."

As I've reflected on that moment over the years, I would phrase it this way: Are you seeking comfort or living for a cause? It would be nice to do both; or to seek a comfortable cause. But often God calls us out of our comfort zone into a cause that challenges and stretches us.

Comfort or cause applies to churches, organizations, business, and individuals. It's a good measuring stick to use when evaluating an idea: Is this about being comfortable or tackling a cause?

REFLECT AND GROW

1. When was the last time you were stretched outside of your comfort zone?

   _____

   _____

   _____

   _____

   _____

   _____

2. What did you learn about yourself?

   _____

   _____

   _____

   _____

   _____

REFLECTIONS

Years ago I read "Renewing Your Spiritual Passion" by Gordon MacDonald. One of the points he emphasizes is the need for rest and reflection if we are to stay spiritually healthy.
God understood this when he created the Sabbath. Jesus modeled it to his disciples by getting up early to pray.

The rest of us struggle to find a balance. Or, if we do find time to rest we forget to reflect. We don't ask questions like ... "Why am I here?" "Am I being a good steward of my life?" "What one thing do I need to do different?"

Reflection may not come naturally to us. We live busy lives and fill our time doing busy things. Busyness does not lead to godliness, however.

I've been reflecting lately, mostly in the early morning hours before everyone else gets up. I fix coffee, listen to music, and pray. And listen. What is God trying to tell me? What does he want me to know?

I don't profess to know the exhaustive answer to those questions. I do believe he wants me to be a good steward of the time and talents he has granted me. There are times when I feel like a poor steward, reacting to the circumstances of life rather than creating them.

Sometimes a growing frustration can be a sign that friction is coming from being out of alignment. Other times it might be last night's dinner.

When I am being a good steward of my time and talents, I feel very much aligned. I'm reminded of Eric Liddell's line in Chariot's of Fire: "When I run I feel the pleasure of

God." I know when those times are in my life. I know when I feel it and when I don't.

We need to reflect at both times. I need to reflect at both times.

REFLECT AND GROW

1. When is your regular time of rest?

   _____

   _____

   _____

   _____

   _____

   _____

   _____

   _____

Chasing Rabbits

I'm not sure who first coined the phrase "chasing rabbits" but it likely wasn't a rabbit lover.

With the exception of those who hunt little bunnies, "chasing rabbits" typically refers to those who prefer to get lost on a tangent rather than staying the course. It's why people get so worked up over minor issues while the major issues are ignored.

Rabbit chasers drive counselors crazy. Rather than deal with the root of a problem, they prefer to hack away at the branches. You might say, "Let's talk about …" and the response is, "but I want to talk about …"

Sometimes employees will become rabbit chasers because it's easier to distract than accept responsibility. Back in my marketplace days, I noticed that under-performing employees had a wonderful gift of recognizing where other people were under-performing, too. Somehow they felt by raising awareness of other's shortcoming it made their own seem less important.

Not all rabbit chasing is malicious. Many a good leader has put mission and vision on the back-burner (or at least a side-burner) and chased a rabbit. That's the curse of the "latest and greatest." It's tempting to always be looking for the new, new thing.

Politicians, especially the experienced ones, know that chasing a rabbit can be dangerous to their electability and it's why they stay on point. It's why when they're asked a question about world peace they usually say something like, "That's a good question, Bob. But the important thing is to get this economy back to work." And they never say a word about world peace. They refuse to chase the rabbit.

Have you been rabbit chasing lately?

REFLECT AND GROW

1. Why is it easy to chase rabbits?

   _____
   _____
   _____
   _____
   _____
   _____
   _____
   _____
   _____
   _____

More And Less

The secret to growth and maturity is not a "more or less" attitude but a "more and less" attitude. For example …

- I need to more focused on the needs of my family and less focused on my own.
- I need to more concerned with what people receive from my preaching and less concerned about how I deliver it.
- I need to spend more time on what's important and less time on what's urgent.

More and less.

Reflect and Grow

1. What do you need to have more of right now?

   _____
   _____
   _____
   _____
   _____

2. What do you need less of?

_____

_____

_____

_____

_____

_____

_____

_____

_____

_____

_____

_____

Success And Significance

Over the last two weeks I've had several conversations with guys who are assessing where they find themselves in life. While "helping" them, I've found it to be helpful myself. How often is that the case!

In my own life, I have a growing uneasiness about spinning my wheels. Let me rephrase that: I have no desire to spin my wheels. Life is too short and too uncertain to just go through the motions.

For me, it's a matter of stewardship. Am I being a good steward of the time and talents God has given me? Sorry to tell you this, but my time (and your time) is only getting shorter. The amount of time I have to make a dent in eternity is less with each moment.

When we arrive in heaven, God will not ask us how we "killed time". He will ask you if you did the best you could with what he gave you. I want to be able to say that I put it out there – that I left nothing on the table.

Honestly, I don't feel that way right now. Don't confuse busyness with effectiveness.

Are you chasing success or significance? Both? Neither?

Reflect and Grow

1. If you were to be honest, are you chasing success or significance?

   _____

2. How do you know if you're being a good steward of your time and talents?

That The Necessary May Speak

I'm reading "The Presentation Secrets of Steve Jobs" and loved this quote in the chapter on simplicity:

"The ability to simplify means to eliminate the unnecessary so that the necessary may speak." – Hans Hoffman, German painter

This is especially true in preaching. The overriding concern in preaching is not to overwhelm our audience with words but to speak the right word at the right time. Transformation is the goal. If we pack too much into a single message, even good stuff, the overall transformational effect will be reduced.

Why?

As painful as this is to admit as a preacher ... They won't remember much of what you say.

If your talk, presentation, or sermon is filled with unnecessary words, strip them out. Only then will you give the necessary words a fighting chance to be heard.

Reflect and Grow

1. As a leader, what are the "necessary words" you don't want others to miss?

_____

Compass Not A Clock

In ministry we talk in terms of a "calling."

A person may be called to youth ministry or working with the poor. A calling is a divine placement upon a person's life. It's passion and purpose wrapped up in one.

Here's another way of thinking about it: people who are living and functioning out of a sense of calling are following their compass and not watching a clock. They live with a sense of direction.

Reflect and Grow

1. Do you believe you have a calling? If so, what is it?

   _____
   _____
   _____
   _____
   _____
   _____
   _____

2. If you're not sure, how will you find one?

Humility

Of all the sessions at the 2011 Willow Creek Leadership Summit, the one by John Dickinson may have been my favorite. An Australian, which gives him an automatic advantage due to a cool accent, Dickinson spoke powerfully on the topic of humility.

First take home: humility makes the great greater.

Here are the five reasons he shared as to why we should cultivate humility.

1. **Humility is common sense**. In short, none of us is an expert on everything. Leaders have to fight the temptation to believe that expertise in one area automatically transfers to another area.

2. **Humility is beautiful**. We are more attracted to the great who are humble than those who are great and know it.

3. **Humility is generative**. Humility generates new knowledge, new abilities. A humble person is willing to learn; the proud already know it.

4. **Humility is persuasive**. The most believable person in the world is the one you know has your best interest at heart.

5. **Humility is inspiring**. When leaders are aloof, we may admire them but we don't emulate them. When great leaders are approachable, we don't just admire them — we aspire to be like them.

REFLECT AND GROW

1. How would you define humility?

   _____

   _____

   _____

   _____

   _____

2. What other reason for cultivating humility would you add to the above list?

   _____

   _____

   _____

   _____

   _____

THE BEST IDEAS

In business, we often hear people talk about "empowerment." The idea is simple: as a leader, you have given power and discretion to your followers to make decisions on their own. Rather than becoming a bottleneck, an empowering leader allows the gifts and talents of his or her team to flow throughout the organization.

How can you tell when empowerment is happening? One symptom that empowerment is a value and not just a buzzword is this: not all the best ideas belong to the leader. This not only relieves the leader of having to be an idea factory, it also allows the team to grow and expand.

The opposite of empowerment is control. Are there things that a leader must control? Absolutely. But not everything.

Where do the best ideas in your organization come from?

REFLECT AND GROW

1. How do leaders disempower their followers?

   _____

   _____

   _____

2. What is one thing you could do to be more empowering at work?

_____

_____

_____

_____

_____

_____

_____

_____

_____

_____

_____

Leadership Agility

In their book, "The Truth About Leadership," authors Jim Kouzes and Barry Pozner write about *leadership agility*. They define leadership agility as the ability to learn and adapt on the fly. Leaders who lack agility are rigid, locked-in to methods that may not work any more. Or they may hold values that are detrimental rather than helpful.

As you lead, you will encounter challenges, difficulties, and setbacks. Agile leaders are learners as well. They learn from what they experiences, in order to improve the next time.

Do you have leadership agility?

Reflect and Grow

1. Describe a time when you lost your mobility?

    _____

    _____

    _____

    _____

    _____

2. In your own situation, what does leadership agility look like?

_____

_____

_____

_____

_____

_____

_____

_____

_____

_____

_____

Something Special

Here's a fundamental belief I have as a pastor: people want to be involved in something special. Whether or not it is unique is not the issue. What matters is this ... are we making a difference?

What makes something "special"? Here are few random thoughts:

- **It goes beyond what is acceptable.** People are not inspired when they are asked to just get by or be mediocre. People are most fulfilled when they are challenged to succeed.
- **It touches the heart.** Meaning comes in different forms for different people. Good leaders are those who help attach meaning to even the simplest task or responsibility. If it's just a job, it's probably not that special.
- **It has the faith factor.** Special projects or special teams have this in common: there is an element of "what are we doing!" "How can we do this?" "Are we crazy?"

Are you creating special opportunities for those you lead?

Reflect and Grow

1. How are you creating a special work environment?

   _____

_____

_____

_____

_____

_____

_____

2. Where you lead, what would it look like to "touch the heart"?

_____

_____

_____

_____

_____

_____

_____

_____

Action And Despair

"Action is the antidote to despair." — Joan Baez, singer-songwriter

Desperation can have a paralyzing effect on us. We might feel surrounded by our circumstances, unable to find the proverbial "light at the end of the tunnel." Sensing no hope, we become immobilized — thinking there is nothing we can do.

We look at the high numbers of children in foster care and wonder, "What can one person or family do?"

We see the faces of poverty and feel poor in our ability to do something.

It might be our own financial situation or a difficult season with a child. When a problem moves from an annoyance to a nuisance to an albatross … we're closer to despair.

Joan Baez is right: action is the antidote to despair.

Often when we take action, even a small action, we begin to feel better. We might not be able to feed the world, but we can feed one person. And that's how change begins. Hope rekindles. Despair starts to evaporate.

So when you sense yourself moving closer to despair, do something, anything. Take action!

REFLECT AND GROW

1. What causes you to feel despair?

   _____

   _____

   _____

   _____

   _____

2. What is one action you can take today to make a positive difference?

   _____

   _____

   _____

   _____

   _____

   _____

Staying Positive

When life gets difficult or challenging, it's important we work extra hard to stay positive. Here are a few things I've found to be helpful.

Get Moving

Inertia is generally bad, especially when it comes to problem-solving. Changing your mood or outlook may be as simple as changing your posture — getting off your behind and moving around.

Change Windows

The same office may have two windows: one opens to the wall of another building and the other has a view of the ocean (or hills or golf course, take your pick).

Most every situation or circumstance we find ourselves in also have multiple windows. Discouragement or despair may mean you need to change windows. Without leaving the room — or situation — you can see things differently.

Walk Together

It's no secret that we weren't made to live or work in isolation. With the exception of cats, most pets even know that.

The beauty of working as a team is that we will be in different emotional states. When one is down, it's likely someone else will be up. When properly assembled, teams complement one another, making us stronger together than we could be individually.

Back to Basics

When we wander too far from the basics, it's easy to get trapped in a never-ending cycle of bigger, better, and faster. Bigger, better, and faster may be nice — even necessary — but they can also be draining. Discouragement sets in when we realize we've lost sight of what's really important.

Every leader needs to know what the basics are that provide for growth and effectiveness and then return to them periodically. It's also one of the best gifts we can give those we lead.

Change Your Focus

We all hit speed bumps in the path of life or business or ministry. An occasional bump is OK; when they come at you in rapid succession, it's easy to get discouraged.

One way to remain positive when you find yourself in a season of testing or trial is this: change your focus. It's too easy to focus on the speed bump and forget that there's an entire road ahead. In fact, there's more than just the road ... there's landscape and scenery and other stuff to look at, too.

REFLECT AND GROW

1. From the above list, which one resonates the most with you?

   _____

_____

_____

_____

_____

_____

2. What have you found that helps you stay positive?

_____

_____

_____

_____

_____

_____

_____

_____

Duplicators Not Doers

For any organization to remain healthy, grow, and expand, the leadership must be about duplication — the art of equipping others to do the work of ministry as God has gifted them. The temptation most leaders face is to be doers, not duplicators.

It might stem from insecurity ("What if they do it better?") or pride ("I'm the only one who can do it right"). Either way, being a doer stunts the organization by capping the growth at the ceiling of our individual abilities.

Are you a duplicator or doer?

Reflect and Grow

1. Why is it easy to be a doer?

   _____
   _____
   _____
   _____
   _____
   _____

2. How can you spot a duplicator?

Sundials In The Shade

Marcus Buckingham says that the most ineffective staff people are like "sundials in the shade." It's not a matter of ability or talent or desire. The real question is this: do we have them in the right role?

As you lead teams of people — be that at church, work, or home — one of your primary tasks is to help place people in the right positions. Whenever talent is misaligned, no one is happy. In fact, misplaced talent will eventually erode if it's not being continually sharpened or utilized.

Do you have any sundials in the shade?

Reflect and Grow

1. What are signs that someone might be in the wrong position?

   _____
   _____
   _____
   _____
   _____
   _____

2. How can you help a person get realigned?

_____

_____

_____

_____

_____

_____

_____

_____

_____

_____

_____

What Else Is Not Enough

"It's in Apple's DNA that technology alone is not enough — it's technology married with liberal arts, married with the humanities, that yields us the result that makes our heart sing." – Steve Jobs, Apple CEO, as quoted by TechCrunch

That's an interesting but insightful statement from a technology company. It recognizes that technology is not simply utilitarian but humanitarian as well — it interacts with people, impacts people, and inspires people.

But what about you? In your life, marriage, business, or team ... what is not enough by itself?

Having spent twenty-plus years as a pastor, I've seen churches that believe right doctrine alone is enough. Or a certain worship style is enough. The list of "enoughs" in the church world is more than I can list in one article.

Here's how you might hear it: "If we just did ___, that would be enough."

Here's what a person is really saying: "If we could find the magic bullet, everything else would fall into place."

Success, health, effectiveness often don't rise or fall on one single ingredient. Rather, they are a combination of marriages ... technology married with a human perspective, beliefs married to behaviors, diet married to exercise. On we could go.

When you find yourself tempted to look for the one magic bullet, don't.

REFLECT AND GROW

1. How can you tell when you are searching for a magic bullet?

   _____

   _____

   _____

   _____

   _____

   _____

   _____

   _____

   _____

   _____

Adjustments And Alignment

I'm sitting in Starbucks enjoying a hot cup of coffee and I'm not sure which I'm most thankful for — the coffee or the ability to sit and type.

One month ago I hurt my hip while playing a game of pick-up basketball. I'd like to say that I landed wrong after slamming a dunk. Truth be told, I simply got knocked down and landed on my kiester. That allowed me to get reacquainted with my sciatic nerve.

For the last three weeks, I've been visiting a chiropractor. He has patiently explained things to me, twisted me further than I've been twisted before, and is getting me back on the straight and narrow. And here I am today sitting comfortably and typing away!

The basic principle of chiropractic care (in laymen's terms) is that we all need adjustments to stay in alignment. That same principle is true in other areas of life as well.

- When our relationships are strained, that's a sign they are out of alignment.
- When teams act more like individuals, that's a sign they are out of alignment.
- When our schedules get filled with things that are urgent but not necessarily important, that's a sign they are out of alignment.

On the one hand, you can do nothing. Denial is a strong temptation. Of course, doing nothing is really doing something — just not the right something.

Another option is to continue doing what you've been doing — and settle for the results you've been getting. But it's not that easy. Doing what we've always done may actually make the problem worse.

The best option, and the most painful but rewarding, is to make an adjustment. Do something different.

A good coach will make an adjustment if he sees that a certain play or player isn't working. A good marriage will make an adjustment to become an even better marriage. A good leader is constantly making adjustments, to seize opportunities or avoid pitfalls.

REFLECT AND GROW

1. Do you have someone or something that is out of alignment?

   _____

   _____

   _____

   _____

   _____

   _____

INFLUENCE AND INTEGRITY

Leadership has been rightly defined as influence. Paraphrasing John Maxwell, if you think you are leading people but no one is following you, you're just taking a walk.

Without influence, a person is not a leader.

Without integrity, a person does not have influence.

You can motivate (influence) people out of fear or guilt for only so long. And after a while, the law of diminishing returns kicks-in and it actually becomes counter-productive. Leaders who use fear to get things done are developing followers who will grow resentful.

Leaders with integrity know that character matters more than competency. Ideally, a leader will have both. But if I had to choose between a leader with high character and average competency or high competency and average character ... It's a no-brainer. Choose otherwise and you're setting yourself up for disappointment; or worse, disaster.

REFLECT AND GROW

1. Describe how integrity and influence work together?

   _____

   _____

   _____

FEAR OF FAILING

Is the fear of failing the greatest when just starting out or after a season of success?

While it is true that a fear of failing may discourage some folks from ever trying anything new, most people eventually do.

A more insidious form of fear comes when a person experiences success. It may be the fear of having to sustain a level of effort required to maintain success. It could be the fear of having to replicate a prior success but in a new environment (economy, personnel changes). Often it is the fear of losing what took hard work to attain.

This fear of failing, rather than discouraging the first step, discourages the next step. It leads to maintenance thinking — what must I/we do to keep the wheels rolling?

Here's the irony: those who have taken the first step and experienced success should have a track record to fall back on. Those who have never taken the first step are truly stepping out in faith.

If you find yourself paralyzed by success, get moving again!

REFLECT AND GROW

1. List a few symptoms of maintenance thinking:

   _____

_____

_____

_____

_____

_____

_____

2. How can you overcome the fear of failing?

_____

_____

_____

_____

_____

_____

_____

Clarity And Communication

One of the things I've learned as a parent that has impacted my effectiveness as a pastor is this: Unless the other person understands what I'm saying, I haven't communicated. I've just been talking.

While talking might make me feel better, it alone does nothing to solve a problem or move the ball forward. Understanding is what matters. My goal in preaching is not to use a certain amount of words; it is to move the listener into closer alignment with God.

As a leader, the same is true. I will gladly sacrifice eloquence for understanding. And one of the most important keys to understanding is being clear about what you're communicating. A lack of clarity allows an issue to get out of focus. It blurs the lines around the action required. It may actually demotivate someone from taking any action at all.

Reflect and Grow

1. When it comes to communicating, what could you to be clearer?

   _____

   _____

   _____

2. How can you tell when a message needs to be clearer?

Shrinking Thinking

Leaders who excel at moving organizations forward (be it a church, business, or team) are typically "big picture" thinkers. By painting a compelling vision of the future, they encourage others to follow where they might not otherwise go. Often it is the leader's ability to begin with the end in mind that gathers people to the vision itself.

As leaders, we need to be aware of what I call "shrinking thinking." Symptoms include focusing on the minutia rather than the mission or reducing options rather than expanding them. A sure sign of a lost vision is when a leader spends too much time wading through the trivial instead of allowing others to handle the details. With that comes a lack of clarity that slows everything down.

The cure?

Set aside significant time each week to reflect on the big picture. And then ask others you trust how big they think it is. If what you think is big is really little, keep burrowing in until you recapture a vision worth living (and dying) for.

Reflect and Grow

1. How would you define your big picture?

    _____

    _____

    _____

2. List one thing to avoid that leads to shrinking thinking?

Simple Enough

One of the challenges of the creative process — be it writing, designing, or speaking — is making complex things simple. Clarity comes with simplicity. And with clarity comes a better chance at persuasion.

The authors of Creative Boldness write:

"A big part of getting to what matters in an idea is simplicity. But it's important that our planners understand the difference between simple and simple enough. In the words of someone handsome and famous, 'Not as few words as possible. As few words as necessary.'"

When crafting a speech, is it simple enough to communicate your message clearly and in a compelling fashion? In designing a print piece, is it simple enough to get your message across?

Reflect and Grow

1. What are the enemies of simplicity?

    _____

    _____

    _____

    _____

Mobility

For the past week or so my right hip has been hurting – to the point that it is hard to get in/out of bed and move in certain directions. Sitting for long periods of time means standing up with a sharp pain and a stiff leg. Jumping up and down is out of the question!

When the body is functioning normal, we take our mobility for granted. Getting out of bed doesn't require a strategy; you just do it. It's amazing how vital mobility is to having an enjoyable afternoon or even a productive walk to the kitchen.

The part week has made me think about a different kind of mobility ... the ability to quickly adapt your thinking and attitude to changing circumstances. I'm not suggesting moral relativism – truth is truth regardless of our situation or circumstances. But what about our perspective on disappointments? Or how we handle challenges? Or see opportunities? Or view our potential?

When it comes to matters of attitude, many people are paralyzed by immobility. They simply can't (or won't) move in a better direction or a different direction.

An immobile attitude may see an opportunity through the lens of a previous failure. Fear of failure can stiffen mental joints. It's also possible to be paralyzed by success. Every new opportunity is seen as extension of what worked in the past. New realities may not be considered.

A mobile attitude is a curious attitude. It seeks to learn and explore. It is willing to take action, even if it is a small step.

Perhaps the worst part of mental immobility is that we may not know we suffer from it. Unlike my right hip which sends a pain signal to my brain every time I move it, mental stiffness sends no immediate warning signal. The absence of pain, however, is not necessarily an indication of health.

So, don't take your mobility for granted. Exercise your right to move.

REFLECT AND GROW

1. How can you improve your curiosity?

    _____

    _____

    _____

    _____

    _____

    _____

    _____

COURAGE

"I learned that courage was not the absence of fear, but the triumph over it. The brave man is not the one who does not feel afraid, but who conquers fear." - Nelson Mandela.

This from a man who spent 27 years in a South African prison for standing up against apartheid – racial inequalities.

Growth in life is not the absence of pivotal circumstances. It is the result of allowing God to work in those circumstances.

The most pivotal circumstance in all of history was when Jesus prayed before going to the cross. Not my will but yours be done.

We can overcome our pivotal circumstances because Jesus faced his.

REFLECT AND GROW

1. What have you discovered helps you overcome fear?

   _____

   _____

   _____

_____

_____

_____

2. What current or upcoming situation to need to be prepared for?

_____

_____

_____

_____

_____

_____

_____

_____

Developing Spiritual Wisdom

If only getting wise was as simple as getting older.

I didn't ask for gray hairs — I simply had children! My knees decided on their own how much basketball I would be able to play in one week. Aging happens; wisdom is not so automatic.

How does a person gain spiritual wisdom? When the apostle Paul writes his letter to the Colossians, he shares this prayer:

"For this reason, since the day we heard about you, we have not stopped praying for you. We continually ask God to fill you with the knowledge of his will through all the wisdom and understanding that the Spirit gives, so that you may live a life worthy of the Lord and please him in every way ..." (Colossians 1:9-10).

The Holy Spirit grants wisdom to those who yield themselves to God. There are certain things we can only learn or understand by doing. Faith is one of those things.

Until Peter stepped out of the boat and actually walked on water (Matthew 14), he may have intellectually believed it was possible to walk on water with God's help. Having seen Jesus do it himself, he may have developed a good theory. At that point, he had belief — but did he have faith?

Peter gained spiritual wisdom and understanding only when his foot struck the water and he didn't sink. It was at that point that theory became reality.

As you experience God's faithfulness your own faith in him grows. If you want to learn more of the Bible, try teaching it to four and five year-olds. If you want to develop a faith that believes God will provide for your needs, start a new church without a building or budget.

It is when you take a faith-inspired action that your spiritual wisdom and understanding grows. Which, in turn, grows your faith.

REFLECT AND GROW

1. What is the difference between wisdom and knowledge?

    _____

    _____

    _____

    _____

    _____

    _____

    _____

Watching And Listening

When it comes to effective communication, we've all been told that we need to be good listeners. If we were listening, then we know that. But there's another part of communication that often gets overlooked: watching.

A good communicator will not only listen to the other party but will watch them, too. Non-verbal cues may help you understand what the other person is really thinking, not just what they are saying.

Listen and watch. A good combination.

Reflect and Grow

1. What are ways that people communicate non-verbally?

   _____

   _____

   _____

   _____

   _____

   _____

   _____

2. How can you improve your listening and watching skills?

_____

_____

_____

_____

_____

_____

_____

_____

_____

_____

_____

Great People, Great Passion

Dwight Moody was one of the most successful evangelists of the 19th century — despite the fact he didn't have much of an education. Several British ministers once asked him why he had been so effective.

Moving to his hotel window, Moody asked them what they saw outside. Across the way was a city park and all Moody's guests agreed they saw people.

With tears in his eyes, Moody responded, "But I see countless souls who will one day spend eternity in hell if they do not find their Savior."

Great men are filled with great passions.

Reflect and Grow

1. What are you passionate about?

   _____

   _____

   _____

   _____

   _____

2. When was the last time something moved you to tears? Why?

_____

_____

_____

_____

_____

_____

_____

_____

_____

_____

_____

_____

_____

Carving Out The Angel

I came across this quote from Michelangelo, the great Italian artist, about how he approached his art: ***"I saw the angel in the marble and carved until I set him free."***

- All great musicians hear the music before they write the music.

- All great film makers can see the movie before they start shooting.

- All great leaders see the potential within those they lead.

Jesus looked at Simon — the impetuous one who walked on water only to sink in doubt — and changes his name to "the Rock", also known as Peter.

You might be surrounded by angels and not know it if you can't see it first.

Reflect and Grow

1. How can you improve your ability to spot angels?

   _____

   _____

   _____

   _____

_____

_____

_____

_____

2. Who is one potential leader you can invest time in?

_____

_____

_____

_____

_____

_____

_____

LEADERSHIP AND BELIEF

How do you motivate people? If you are a parent, how do you inspire your child to tackle greater challenges? If you are a boss, how do you get employees to produce consistent results?

While there are many answers to the question of motivation, I'd like to focus on just one: belief. Not belief in terms of a "set of beliefs" or dogmas or even convictions.

But belief in this sense: people want someone to believe in and they want someone to believe in them.

Children desperately need someone to believe in. They need someone to look up to. They need someone who will model for them the right values. They crave consistency.

As they grow up in a world that is constantly changing they also need a steady presence that will reassure them, console them, even confront them when necessary. In short, when they go through a season of self-doubt (as most kids do), that's when they need a parent to believe in them.

Adults are no different. In fact, they may be harder to lead because they apply a more rigorous sniff test.

Employees, players, co-workers ... everyone is motivated by following someone they can believe in. This means being honest about the risks and rewards, as well as modeling the behavior one is asking from another.

And they need someone who will believe in them. Adult don't need cheerleaders; they do need, however, someone who will draw out the best they have to offer. This may mean coaching them when necessary. It may also mean releasing them fly on their own — even at the risk of failure. If we never let them leave the nest, we may be communicating a lack of belief in their abilities.

If you are a leader, parent, or coach, what are you communicating in regards to belief?

REFLECT AND GROW

1. Who was the first person to believe in you?

   _____

   _____

   _____

   _____

   _____

   _____

   _____

Motivating Employees

How do you create a work environment that brings out the best in people, accomplishes great things, and doesn't require sending all your employees to a Tony Robbins seminar? Here are a few tips.

Let people know if they are meeting expectations. This assumes, of course, that the expectations have been clearly identified, communicated, and accepted. If they have been, leaders owe to those they lead to let them know how they are doing. Unfortunately, many companies wait for the annual review; by this time, many items that could have been fixed with a mid-course corrections have developed into deeper issues.

Be kind to people. Kindness is a sign of respect. Many leaders in the corporate environment equate kindness with softness. It's too "touch feely" to be kind. If you're too kind, people will walk all over you. Nothing could be further from the truth. When people know you truly care about them, they will walk over hot coals for you. Kindness could be a gentle word, a hand-written note, or simply a smile.

Life doesn't revolve around the office only. It may surprise a few bosses to discover that those they lead actually have lives outside of the workplace. A flexible attitude will earn the respect and hard work of others.

REFLECT AND GROW

1. How does the Golden Rule apply to work environments?

   _____

   _____

   _____

   _____

   _____

2. What are signs that an employee may not understand your expectations?

   _____

   _____

   _____

   _____

   _____

Risk And Fear

As anyone who invests in the stock market knows, greater risk equals greater potential. That potential could be a huge return or a colossal failure. To minimize the potential for loss, one would by necessity reduce the risk involved.

Take this same concept and apply it to innovation.

Truly innovative people and businesses understand that to achieve greater levels of creativity requires a high tolerance for risk. As John Ortberg once wrote, to walk on water one must get out of the boat. This involves risk. You might sink! The product you launch might fail. Your illustration might bomb.

Attached to risk is fear. We are afraid of what we don't know or don't understand. We are afraid of failing. So what do some folks do? To reduce fear, they reduce risk. It's natural. But it's not the best route to innovation.

Safety and creativity don't necessarily go hand-in-hand. It's not that we throw caution to the wind and do something we know is utterly stupid and dangerous; but there are times when we step out of the boat not seeing where our foot might land.

Reflect and Grow

1. How is your tolerance for risk?

   _____

   _____

2. Describe the relationship between fear and innovation:

Wannabee, Knowitall, Or Sponge

Which kind of leader are you?

The Wannabee. This person wants to be a leader or an entrepreneur or a church planter or a ... fill in the blank. Why? Because it's the cool thing to do. It's trendy. The wannabee doesn't have a personal sense of mission that is driving his or her decisions. Without a deeply-felt sense of purpose, the wannabee drifts from conference to conference looking for what is currently in style.

The Knowitall. Most of us have known a know-it-all. This is the person who has an answer to everything and therefore doesn't seek out the answers of others. The knowitall already has it figured out. What may be projected as confidence is really insecurity — and a fear that they will be found out. At the root of the knowitall is pride and an emphasis on "I".

The Sponge. How can you discern a sponge from a wannabee or knowitall? It's easy: listen to who does most of the talking. A sponge learns by listening. They absorb and observe. A sponge asks questions. They read. They surround themselves with smart people and let them do their jobs. If pride is the driving factor behind a wannabee or knowitall, humility characterizes the sponge.

So, which kind of leader will you be?

REFLECT AND GROW

1. What attracts the wannabees?

   _____

   _____

   _____

   _____

   _____

   _____

2. How can you become more spongy?

   _____

   _____

   _____

   _____

   _____

   _____

Vision Casting And Bubbling

As leaders, we often think in terms of vision casting. It's our responsibility to discern where God wants us to go and then to paint the picture for those we lead. In many respects, this is a top-down process. We hear from God, our churches/members/employees hear from us.

I also believe part of our mandate as leaders is to help bubble up vision from within the hearts of those we lead. God doesn't speak only to me; he is constantly at work in our world to establish his kingdom. As a leader, I need to be sensitive to what God is saying to those around me.

What are their dreams? What inspires them? What is gaining momentum in their lives?

Casting vision isn't always about shouting from the rooftops; it's just as often about keeping an ear to the ground.

Reflect and Grow

1. When was the last time you asked an employee or coworker about their dreams?

   _____

   _____

   _____

   _____

2. How can you keep an ear to the ground?

How Can We Vs. Why Did You

One of the most important parts of being a coaching leader is learning to ask the right questions.

Here's a good example. If something doesn't out the way it was supposed to, do you ask "Why did you …?" This immediately puts the other person on the defensive and back-pedaling people can be dangerous people.

A better question might be, "How can we …?" This invites a solution rather than placing blame. It also involves the leader in helping ascertain the solution.

Reflect and Grow

1. Which question do you most often ask?

   _____

   _____

   _____

   _____

   _____

   _____

   _____

2. What is the power behind asking, "How can we" questions?

Leadership Seasons

One of the things I enjoy about living in Colorado is the changing of seasons. Don't get me wrong: having an average daily temperature of 70.5 degrees (as we did in **San Diego**) is not all that bad. But I enjoy the turning of leaves, a crisp morning, and a fireplace at a night. I'm not necessarily a big fan of shoveling snow – nor do I expect it to grow on me.

Just as the world around us goes through seasons, we experience seasons in life. It might generational seasons, such as youth, adolosence, middle age, etc. It might life-stages such as marriage, parenting, or retirement.

Spiritually-speaking, seasons may come in the form of dry bouts where we pray but nothing seems to happen. Or it could be a season of growth, a time of seeing God work in ways we never imagined.

Leadership has its seasons, too.

Any leader who has led for any length of time knows there will be different seasons. Tests, challenges, opportunities, conflicts, uncertainties, wins, losses, regrouping. The test of a leader is how they navigate the different seasons. A season of opportunity may require a different speed and mindset than a season of challenge or change.

When the going is good, we may be lulled into thinking the season will last forever. And when it is a season of testing, it is good to remind ourselves it is just that — only a season.

It's important to learn the rhythm of the different seasons. Will it begin with a burst? End with a bang? Encounter expected road bumps of opposition or resistance? While the rhythms may vary, there is usually a certain consistent tone to the melody.

While not all seasons are equally enjoyable, they may be equally important. A season of growth fuels further growth and optimism; a season of challenge may strengthen convictions.

In the end, seasons change. As leaders, so do we.

REFLECT AND GROW

1. What season of leadership are you in right now?

   _____

   _____

   _____

   _____

   _____

   _____

Are You Running Aimlessly?

When was the last time you decided to go for a run without any thought of where you would go?

"That day, for no particular reason, I decided to go for a little run. So I ran to the end of the road. And when I got there, I thought maybe I'd run to the end of the town. And when I got there, I thought maybe I'd just run across Greenbow County. And I figured, since run this far, maybe I'd just run across the great state of Alabama. And that's what I did. I ran clear across Alabama. For no particular reason I just kept on goin'. I ran clear to the ocean. And when I got there, I figured, since I'd gone this far, I might as well turn around, just keep on goin'. When I got to another ocean, I figured, since I'd gone this far, I might as well just turn back, keep right on going." — Forrest Gump

Though I think Forrest and the apostle Paul would agree about "stupid is as stupid does", Forrest's running philosophy would have driven the apostle Paul crazy. Listen to Paul's challenge to the Corinthian church (and to us as well):

"Do you not know that in a race all the runners run, but only one gets the prize? Run in such a way as to get the prize. Everyone who competes in the games goes into strict training. They do it to get a crown that will not last, but we do it to get a crown that will last forever. Therefore I do not run like someone running aimlessly; I do not fight like a boxer beating the air" ([1 Corinthians 9:24-26](#)).

The whole idea of running aimlessly seems absurd. Why would anyone go to all the effort and exertion of running without some idea of where they would want to end up?

But people run aimlessly all the time, even in dress clothes or blue jeans. They live without a guiding purpose. They act without core principles or values. They change directions due to circumstances rather than convictions.

People who run aimlessly tend to not win the prize, whether that prize be a healthy relationship, a growing church or business, or a closer bond with God.

Maps may change. Life changes. Circumstances change. A compass, however, will always point to true north.

God is looking for people who know how to use a compass.

REFLECT AND GROW

1. Are you running aimlessly or with a compass?

    _____

2. How do you know?

    _____

    _____

    _____

    _____

    _____

Love What You Do and I Might Love It, Too

My oldest daughter, Hannah, and I spent a few days in Nashville visiting colleges. Yes, it's hard to believe in one year she will be off to college … somewhere. So, we're doing the college tour routine: Schedule a visit, sit through a presentation, and take a walking tour.

In Nashville, we had the opportunity to tour three schools: Lipscomb, Belmont, and Vanderbilt. Also known as pricey, pricier, and priciest.

While I had grown up in the same church tradition as Lipscomb, I had never actually visited the campus until this week. I was pleasantly surprised by the campus (though I'm not exactly sure why I was surprised that it would have a nice campus). On the walking tour, I even passed an old acquaintance — Keith Lancaster, of Acappella fame. Hannah was given a free t-shirt (swag!) at the end and so we picked up a t-shirt for Hope that says "Lipscomb Softball" (their team recently made the NCAA tournament).

Next, we went to Belmont and did the tour. The first thing we noticed were the huge, beautiful buildings and trees. Lots of trees. Our tour guide walked backwards the entire way, somehow avoiding fountains and curbs. Belmont is known for its quality music program, which is no surprise given its location in Nashville. We left Belmont with no swag in hand.

Our third stop was Vanderbilt. I had never been to Vanderbilt either and thought, "Hey, we're in Nashville for a few days. Let's go see Vandy." Of the three schools,

Vanderbilt (by far) has the largest and prettiest campus. It has everything a three billion dollar endowment can buy. For this tour, our guide was an engineering student who actually enjoyed talking to live people. Before we left, we went to the college bookstore and purchased our own swag.

Here are my reflections as they relate to the process and the impact.

- At Lipscomb, it was an admissions presentation first, tour second.
- At Belmont, it was a tour first, admissions presentation second.
- At Vanderbilt, it was an admissions presentation first, tour second.

I think Lipscomb and Vanderbilt did it right: hit you with the presentation first and let your last impression be of the campus. Parents want the facts and figures but kids are interested in how the campus "feels".

Both Lipscomb and Vanderbilt had admissions representatives who were former students and not just hired professionals. This was evident in how they talked about their experience with the schools. They often referred to what they did as students, how the school had impacted them personally, etc. The Belmont rep probably did more to DISCOURAGE us away from Belmont than to move us TOWARDS Belmont. I went to Belmont *really, really* wanting to like it and how the session ended *really* disappointed me. The admission rep was a nice fellow, and would have been fine in a meeting with just parents or kids already sold on going to Belmont. But if you were new or undecided, the last session was counter-productive.

All three schools used current students to conduct the tours. This made sense and all three did a fantastic job. Again, the personal side came out and added color commentary to the experience.

From a marketing and communications perspective, Vanderbilt was the top and Lipscomb a close second. Unfortunately, I felt like Belmont was a distant third. To be fair, both Lipscomb and Belmont had far fewer students on the tour than Vanderbilt (Vanderbilt had at least 40 students, Belmont had 6, and Lipscomb had 2). I know from a communications standpoint, it's often harder to present to a smaller crowd than a larger crowd.

At Lipscomb, it was just the two families sitting in a room — informally — and it was a great opportunity to talk to the rep about various things. She was friendly, upbeat, and spoke highly of her Lipscomb experience.

At Vanderbilt, the rep did an outstanding job presenting her school and keeping us engaged. She was funny, quirky but not odd, self-effacing, and polished. As we were leaving for our campus tour, she even remembered that Hannah had introduced herself as being from Colorado — after hearing 40 other students introduce themselves, too.

Here's what both of them had in common along with the student tour guides: they loved what they were doing.

It left me thinking: If you love what you do, there's a good chance I might end up loving it, too.

Think about that.

REFLECT AND GROW

1. How can you tell when a person loves what they do?

   _____

   _____

   _____

   _____

   _____

   _____

   _____

   _____

   _____

   _____

LEADERSHIP IS STEWARDSHIP

At its core, effective leadership is really stewardship.

As the leader of a church, I am not the owner; I am a steward. God has entrusted to me both human and financial resources and expects me to utilize them effectively. As a leader, I will be judged not only by how I used my own resources but also the resources of those around me.

- Did I bring out the best in them?
- Did I allow them to grow and expand?
- Did I encourage their development?
- Did I become a bottleneck, requiring all decisions to flow through me?
- Did I inhibit a good idea simply because it wasn't mine?

REFLECT AND GROW

1. How would thinking of leadership as stewardship change the way you lead?

   _____
   _____
   _____

Soaring with the Eagles

In one of my sermons, I shared several demotivational slogans from Despair.com. They are parodies of the motivational posters you can hang in your office. One of my favorites was this one:

"Underachievement: Because soaring with the eagles requires so much more effort."

As funny as that it is, it's also true. Because achievement, effectiveness, and success require work, there are some who opt to underachieve. It's easier to be average.

Coaches who turnaround losing teams understand that it requires more — not less — work.

Breakthrough leaders in any field have a low tolerance for quitting.

Artists or engineers who pursue excellence do so knowing that it comes with a cost.

As hard as it might be, when you reach cruising altitude, the view makes the hard work worth the effort.

Reflect and Grow

1. Describe a time when hard work paid off:

   _____

   _____

   _____

_____

_____

_____

_____

_____

2. What did you learn from that experience?

_____

_____

_____

_____

_____

_____

_____

Chronic Inconsistency

Jim Collins is one of my favorite authors on business and leadership. I've been reviewing my notes from a talk he gave at the 2012 Willow Creek Global Leadership Summit. He was sharing principles based on his book, "Great by Choice."

This line from my notes jumped out at me: *"The signature of mediocrity is not an unwillingness to change but is chronic inconsistency."*

For the most part, few of us wake up and decide to be mediocre. It's not a typical life aspiration — or shouldn't be!

But when we allow chronic inconsistency to creep into our lives, our routines, our families, our work environment — we are allowing ourselves to become mediocre. Everyone may miss a deadline here or there. We all make mistakes and occasionally exercise poor judgment. Welcome to the human race. Mediocre people, however, are chronically inconsistent. They are known by spurts and bursts. What is predictable about them is their unpredictability.

Chronic inconsistency. The mere thought of being that way scares me. I don't want to be inconsistent, much less chronically inconsistent.

To move away from mediocrity, one must move towards intentionality — become purposeful about upholding values, making decisions, and following through.

Unlike chronic arthritis, there's no over-the-counter pill you can purchase to make you more consistent. A good electronic calendar, an app like Evernote, or just an old-fashioned sticky note might help. But, in the end, it boils down to this: do you want to be known as consistent or inconsistent?

REFLECT AND GROW

1. What creates (or enables) chronic inconsistency?

   _____

   _____

   _____

   _____

   _____

   _____

   _____

LEADERS MAKE OTHERS BETTER

A few days, I was having a conversation with our youngest daughter about her volleyball team. She had signed up to play for her school and was assigned to a team. She wasn't too happy; she didn't think they were all that good.

Not knowing if that were true or not — and not wanting to argue — I simply asked her this question: "What are you going to do to make them better?" To which I added, "That's what leaders do."

It's true. Leaders exist to help other people improve.

A leader looks at a situation and asks, "What can I do to make this better?"

A whiner looks at the same difficult situation and complains, "Why do I have to deal with this?"

A blamer looks at the same problem and says, "Whose fault is this?"

A person in denial wonders, "What is everyone so upset about?"

I was trying to help my daughter understand a very basic principle: you are either part of the problem or part of the solution. Active or passive, positive or negative, you are still a contributor. The question is: What are you choosing to contribute?

If God has placed you in a position of leadership, no matter what it is, then make the people around you better. That's what leaders do.

REFLECT AND GROW

1. Do you believe it is your role or responsibility to help those you lead get better?

   _____

   _____

   _____

   _____

2. Do your actions match your belief?

   _____

   _____

   _____

   _____

   _____

LEARNING TO LEAD

We know that in order to qualify as a leader you must have at least one person following you. Or, as John Maxwell says, if you think you are leading and no one is behind you — you're just taking a walk.

That being said, every good, effective leader has also been a good, effective follower. In fact, I'm not sure you can learn to lead without first learning how to follow.

Before Jesus deployed his apostles to shake up the world, he first invited them to follow him. Then he spent three years with them, allowing them to shadow him around. They learned to lead by learning to follow.

I'm often asked, "How can I become a better leader?"

Yes, you can read more (and you should). Yes, you can attend great seminars and watch TED talks (and you should). But one of the most effective ways to become a better leader is to become a better follower.

Give it a try.

REFLECT AND GROW

1. What is the connection between being a leader and a follower?

   _____

   _____

   _____

Incarnate or Duplicate?

The person who invented the first photocopy machine must have been a creative person. It is quite a thing to visualize and conceptualize and bring to life a machine that would impact literally millions of lives.

Ironically, the invention of the photocopier has made it easier to duplicate than to innovate. You simply place your paper on the machine and it produces something that looks like the original. With newer technology, it might even look as good as the original — but it is still just a copy.

Photocopiers are not evil (except when they constantly jam and chew up paper). In fact, there are innumerable times when duplication is necessary, even beneficial.

However, I'm thankful that when God responded to our sinful condition, he chose to incarnate rather than duplicate.

God could have duplicated the systems that were already in place, the hundreds of laws passed down throughout Hebrew history.

God could have duplicated the most pious of the priests. He could have copied the handbooks of other religions, even revising and updating them.

Instead, he chose to incarnate himself and the result was Jesus, Emmanuel – God with us. The apostle John puts it this way, "The Word became flesh and made his dwelling among us" (John 1:14). Or, as Eugene Peterson puts it, "he moved into our neighborhood."

But for us humans, this fact remains: it is far easier to duplicate than incarnate.

It is why I love the "cut and paste" feature on my laptop or phone. It saves me from having to retype words or sentences.

"Cut and paste" might be nice feature when you're working on a document, but it is a poor way to live out your mission in life. Yet that is exactly what many people (and churches) do all the time. We find someone who is living passionately and try to mimic their passion, thinking the key must be in the words they use or music they listen to. Church leaders "cut and paste" from the latest conference or book, choosing to duplicate rather than incarnate.

What if you stepped back and asked, "God, what part of your character, your heart, do you want me to incarnate today? How can I put flesh and blood on your truth in my everyday, ordinary life?"

To place a sheet of paper on the copier and make a copy doesn't require big dreams. In fact, duplication often shrinks our dreams.

Incarnation requires God-powered, God-inspired dreams. God is not dead and does not need us to bring him back to life. He is alive. He is big. His dreams are big.

What size are your dreams?

REFLECT AND GROW

1. Why do leaders choose to duplicate someone else's ideas rather than incarnate their own?

   _____

   _____

   _____

   _____

   _____

2. What are the dangers in having a "cut and paste" approach to leading?

   _____

   _____

   _____

   _____

   _____

   _____

Taking the High Road

If you interact with people at any level, there will be times that you will be misunderstood, misrepresented, and even maligned. Believe it or not, people will not always say nice things about you. Most likely, this revelation is not a surprise to you.

As a younger man, I didn't always respond in the best fashion. It was easy to give in the temptation to join the other person in the gutter. That's often what they want you to do. But, as I remember my mom telling me, "Two wrongs don't make a right."

So, what to do? Take the high road.

Taking the high road means you won't wade into the sludge, slinging mud around. Taking the high road means that you won't shred the other person with the truth. Taking the high road means you won't feel the need to defend every misrepresentation or outright lie. Taking the high road means following the command of Peter:

> *"Do not repay evil with evil or insult with insult. On the contrary, repay evil with blessing, because to this you were called so that you may inherit a blessing."* — 1 Peter 3:9

Returning insult with insult is a no-win proposition. It creates a downward spiral. In the end, it simply does not honor Jesus.

This is why the Proverb writer offered this counsel: *"Do not answer a fool according to his folly, or you yourself will be just like him"* (Proverbs 26:4).

Answering a foolish charge may make you feel better, but it may not elevate Jesus. Answering a fool using foolish logic will make you a fool as well.

Taking the high road isn't easy.

It is necessary.

REFLECT AND GROW

1. What helps you take the high road?

   _____
   _____
   _____
   _____
   _____
   _____
   _____
   _____
   _____
   _____

Stopping the Downward Spiral

Groups are susceptible to downward spirals.

Momentum can move in either a positive or negative direction. Thoughts feed off other thoughts. Feelings feed off other feelings. Attitudes are contagious. In a group setting, all it takes is one person to infect the others with a critical spirit. Negativity is like pollution: it's easier to notice when you're visiting from out-of-town than when you live with it everyday. When a team gets stuck in the loop of a downward spiral, it's often easier to continue the slide than to reverse it.

So, how do you stop a downward spiral?

Incrementally. If you find yourself in a downward spiral, introduce something positive to your routine. One slight, positive adjustment alters the course of a meeting or a day. If you don't like the direction you're going, steer a different direction.

Instantly. There are times when a negative environment must be confronted head-on. If a team persists in making critical comments that undermine the morale of other teammates, you might have to say, "That's not an appropriate way to talk."

Preventative. The best way to deal with the downward spiral is to avoid it altogether. Nip negativity in the bud. Put in place a culture that celebrates the good. Emphasize gratitude.

Downward spirals can be reversed. Upward spirals are just as possible as downward ones. Remember, momentum can move in either a positive or negative direction.

REFLECT AND GROW

1. Is there an incremental change you need to make right now?

   _____

   _____

   _____

   _____

2. What is a preventative measure you can take to avoid the downward spiral?

   _____

   _____

   _____

   _____

   _____

Keeping Things in Perspective

For anyone in a leadership position, it is easy to believe the lies of your critics. It is just as easy to believe every good word ever said about you. Neither of which might actually be true.

Norman McGowan in his book, My Years With Winston Churchill, tells the following story.

Winston Churchill was once asked, "Doesn't it thrill you to know that every time you make a speech, the hall is packed to overflowing?" "It's quite flattering," replied Sir Winston. "But whenever I feel that way, I always remember that if instead of making a political speech I was being hanged, the crowd would be twice as big."

Don't believe every critic.

Don't believe all the applause.

Reflect and Grow

1. How do you keep a proper perspective about yourself?

   _____

   _____

   _____

2. What are the dangers in believing the critics?

___

What's Next

Growing leaders in any facet of life are always trying to answer the same question: "What's next?"

During a season of growth, it might be tempting to consider settling down, playing it safe. It might seem reasonable to rest and enjoy. What appears to be a summit may actually be a plateau. A good leader will be thinking ahead ... "What's next?"

When we find ourselves in the midst of a struggle, it's easy to ask "What's next?" and to expect that the answer means a release from our tension and conflict. That may be the answer; it also may not be the answer. The answer may lie in what God wants to teach us during the journey. Emerging stronger, we ask again "What's next?"

Asking "What's next?" keeps us focused on the future — on growing, developing, learning, and maturing.

Reflect and Grow

1. What's next for you?

   _____

   _____

   _____

   _____

   _____

2. What is your first step in that direction?

_____
_____
_____
_____
_____
_____
_____
_____
_____
_____
_____
_____
_____
_____

About the Author

Born and raised in East Peoria, IL, Ken Hensley has suffered from a life-long affinity for the Chicago Cubs. He attributes his longevity in preaching to being well acquainted with suffering, special thanks to the Cubs.

For the past twenty years Ken has served as a senior pastor in San Diego, San Francisco, Atlanta, and Denver. In 2005, he planted a new church in San Diego with Stadia: New Church Strategies. He currently serves as the senior pastor at Mountainview Christian Church.

He and his wife, Tonya, have two daughters and reside in Highlands Ranch, CO.

Get in Touch

Blog: http://www.kenhensley.com

Twitter: @kenhensley

Facebook: facebook.com/kenhensley

www.ingramcontent.com/pod-product-compliance
Lightning Source LLC
Chambersburg PA
CBHW071757200526
45167CB00017B/402